Control the Controller

Understanding and Resolving Video Game Addiction

By Ciaran O'Connor UKCP, MA

First published in 2014 by
Free Publishing Limited

A CIP Catalogue of this book is available from
the British Library

ISBN: 978-1-85343-226-2

Typeset in Janson Text 11pt by
www.chandlerbookdesign.co.uk

Printed in Great Britain by
PrintonDemand-Worldwide

Video Games and Addiction

Dr. Mark D. Griffiths

Director, International Gaming Research Unit, Psychology Division,
Nottingham Trent University, United Kingdom, NG1 4BU

I was delighted to be asked by Ciaran O'Connor to write the 'Foreword' to his new book. As you will soon read, Ciaran had his own issues surrounding gaming addiction and has used his own personal experiences to help underpin his own psychological therapeutic interventions in the treatment of gaming addiction. Ciaran's writing is heartfelt and personal. However, he has also attempted to integrate some of the academic and clinical literature to support his views. He wrote this book because he felt it needed to be written and he wanted others that have or treat (or want to treat) this problem to have a resource they could turn to.

For nearly 30 years I have been studying behavioural addictions (put simply, addictions that don't involve taking any drugs). In the mid-1980s I began my academic career by studying adolescents that were addicted to 'fruit machines' in amusement arcades. It was through this work I began to notice teenagers that would spend all day in the arcade playing on the video game machines. In the early 1990s I began to publish academic papers on video game addiction and saw many similarities (both behaviourally and psychologically) between both playing video games and slot machines. By the mid-1990s, I began researching into 'internet addiction' and in 1995 I published an academic paper simply entitled 'Technological Addictions' in which I brought all these disparate behaviours (video game addiction, internet addiction, television addiction, slot machine addiction, etc.) under one conceptual umbrella. Since then, the field of technological addictions has expanded greatly – particularly in the area of gaming addiction.

Gaming addiction has changed and evolved greatly since I first started researching in the area. In the 1980s, the focus was on arcade video game addiction. In the 1990s, the focus changed to home console video game addiction. Over the last decade, the focus has been online video game addiction – particularly in relation to Massively Multiplayer Online Role Playing Games (such as *World of Warcraft* and *Everquest*). In the 1990s I researched separately into internet addiction and video game addiction but now they have become part of the same area of study.

Over the last 15 years, research into various online addictions has greatly increased. One of the most important consequences of the increased amount of research in this area is that in May 2013, 'Internet Gaming Disorder' was officially recognized by the American Psychiatric Association as an area warranting further research and was included in the appendix of the fifth edition of the Diagnostic and Statistical Manual of Mental Disorders (more popularly known as the DSM-5).

Prior to the publication of the DSM-5 in 2013, there had been some debate as to whether 'internet addiction' should be introduced into the text as a separate disorder. Alongside this, there has also been debate as to whether those researching in the online addiction field should be researching generalized internet use and/or the potentially addictive activities that can be engaged on the internet (e.g., gambling, video gaming, sex, shopping, etc.). Following these debates, the Substance Use Disorder Work Group (SUDWG) recommended that the DSM-5 include a sub-type of problematic internet use (i.e., internet gaming disorder [IGD]) in Section 3 ('Emerging Measures and Models') as an area that needed future research before being included in future editions of the DSM.

According to leading scholars in the area, IGD will not be included as a separate mental disorder until the (i) defining features of IGD have been identified, (ii) reliability and validity of specific IGD criteria have been obtained cross-culturally, (iii) prevalence rates have been determined in representative epidemiological samples across the world, and (iv) etiology and associated biological features have been evaluated.

Although there is now a rapidly growing literature on pathological video gaming, one of the key reasons that IGD was not included in the main text of the DSM-5 was that that there are no standardized diagnostic criteria used to assess gaming addiction across the many studies that have been published. For instance, I (and some of my Australian colleagues) carried out a review of instruments that have been used to assess problematic, pathological and/or addictive gaming. We reported that 18 different screening instruments had been developed, and that these had been used in over 60 quantitative studies comprising nearly 60,000 participants.

The main strengths of these gaming addiction screens included: (i) the brevity and ease of scoring, (ii) excellent psychometric properties such as convergent validity and internal consistency, and (iii) robust data that will aid the development of standardized norms for adolescent populations. However, the main weaknesses identified in the instrumentation included: (i) core addiction indicators being inconsistent across studies, (ii) a general lack of any temporal dimension, (iii) inconsistent cut-off scores relating to clinical status, (iv) poor and/or inadequate inter-rater reliability and predictive validity, and (v) inconsistent and/or dimensionality.

Video gaming that is problematic, pathological and/or addictive lacks a widely accepted definition. I argued in a paper that I co-wrote with some of my Hungarian colleagues that some researchers consider video games as the starting point for examining the characteristics of this specific disorder, while others consider the internet as the main platform that unites different addictive internet activities, including online games. Recent studies have made an effort to integrate both approaches. Consequently, IGD can either be viewed as a specific type of video game addiction, or as a variant of internet addiction, or as an independent diagnosis.

Clinical interventions and treatment for problematic and/or addictive video game play vary considerably in the psychological and medical literature, with most of the very few published studies employing some type of cognitive-behavioural therapy (CBT), pharmacotherapy, and/or self-devised psychological interventions. Currently, the evidence based on the treatment of problematic and/or addictive gaming is limited. Furthermore, the lack of consistent approaches to treating problematic video game playing and video game addiction makes it difficult to produce any definitive conclusions as to the efficacy of treatment, although at this stage CBT (as with the treatment efficacy of other addictions) appears to show good preliminary support. There remains a need for controlled, comparative studies of psychological and pharmacological treatments, administered individually and in combination with each other, to determine the optimal treatment approach.

In South East Asia there appears to be significant demand for treatment for online-related problems including gaming addiction. The South Korean government has reportedly established a network of over 140 counselling centres for treatment of online addiction. In Western countries, gaming addiction clinics have also started to emerge in places such as Holland and the UK. There are also treatment groups that are modelled on 12-step self-help treatment (e.g., Online Gamers Anonymous). However, little detail is known about the treatment protocols or their efficacy.

As you will see later in this book when Ciaran outlines some of my thoughts about addiction, I believe that all addictions share more commonalities than differences (i.e., salience, mood modification, tolerance, withdrawal symptoms, conflict, and relapse), and likely reflect a common etiology of addictive behaviour. Consequently, online game addiction is viewed as a specific type of video game addiction.

Some researchers do not differentiate between problematic video game use and problematic online game use. These scholars conceptualize problematic video game use as excessive use of one or more video games resulting in a preoccupation with and a loss of control over playing video games, and various negative psychosocial and/or physical consequences. However, unlike me, their criteria for problematic video game use does not include other features usually associated with dependence or addiction (e.g., tolerance, physical symptoms of withdrawal), as they say there is no clear evidence that problematic gaming is associated with such phenomena. Other researchers such as Dr. Kimberley Young view online gaming addiction as a sub-type of internet addiction and that the internet itself provides situation-specific characteristics that facilitate gaming becoming problematic and/or addictive.

Irrespective of approach or model, the components and dimensions that comprise online gaming addiction are very similar to the IGD criteria in the DSM-5. For instance, my six addiction components directly map onto the nine proposed criteria for IGD (of which five or more need to be endorsed and resulting in clinically significant impairment). More specifically: (1) *preoccupation with internet games* [salience]; (2) *withdrawal symptoms when internet gaming is taken away* [withdrawal]; (3) *the need to spend increasing amounts of time engaged in internet gaming* [tolerance]; (4) *unsuccessful attempts to control participation in internet gaming* [relapse/loss of control]; (5) *loss of interest in hobbies and entertainment as a result of, and with the exception of, internet gaming* [conflict]; (6) *continued excessive use of internet games despite knowledge of psychosocial problems* [conflict]; (7) *deception of family members, therapists, or others regarding the amount of internet gaming* [conflict]; (8) *use of internet gaming to escape or relieve a negative mood* [mood modification]; and (9) *loss of a significant relationship, job, or educational or career opportunity because of participation in internet games* [conflict].

The fact that IGD was included in the DSM-5 appears to have been well received by researchers and clinicians in the gaming addiction field (and by those individuals that have sought treatment for such disorders and had their experiences psychiatrically validated and feel less stigmatized). However, for IGD to be included in the section on 'Substance-Related and Addictive Disorders' along with 'Gambling Disorder', the gaming addiction field must unite and start using the same assessment measures so that comparisons can be made across different demographic groups and different cultures.

For epidemiological purposes, my Hungarian colleagues have asserted that the most appropriate measures in assessing problematic online use (including internet gaming) should meet six requirements. Any instrument should have: (i) *brevity* (to make surveys as short as possible and help overcome question fatigue); (ii) *comprehensiveness* (to examine all core aspects of PAP gaming as possible); (iii) *reliability and validity across age groups* (e.g., adolescents vs. adults); (iv) *reliability and validity across data collection methods* (e.g., online, face-to-face interview, paper-and-pencil); (v) *cross-cultural reliability and validity*; and (vi) *clinical validation*. They also noted that an ideal assessment instrument should serve as the basis for defining adequate cut-off scores in terms of both specificity and sensitivity. In addition to further epidemiological and clinical research, further research is also needed on the neurobiology of IGD. A systematic review of neuroimaging studies examining internet addiction and IGD that I co-wrote with Dr. Daria Kuss noted that:

"These studies provide compelling evidence for the similarities between different types of addictions, notably substance-related addictions and Internet and gaming addiction, on a variety of levels. On the molecular level, Internet addiction is characterized by an overall reward deficiency that entails decreased dopaminergic activity. On the level of neural circuitry, Internet and gaming addiction lead to neuroadaptation and structural changes that occur as a consequence of prolonged increased activity in brain areas associated with addiction. On a behavioral level, Internet and gaming addicts appear to be constricted with regards to their cognitive functioning in various domains" (p.347).

The good news is that research in the gaming addiction field does appear to be reaching an emerging consensus. Books such as this one by Ciaran will help legitimize the concept of gaming addiction and how to treat it. For those who have problems concerning their gaming, it may not matter whether it's called an addiction, compulsion, obsession or a dependency. In short, they simply want help in overcoming their problematic gaming. This book helps make that goal that little bit easier.

Further reading

American Psychiatric Association (2013) *Diagnostic and Statistical Manual of Mental Disorders – Text Revision (Fifth Edition)*. Washington, D.C.: Author.

Demetrovics, Z., Urbán, R., Nagygyörgy, K., Farkas, J., Griffiths, M. D., Pápay, O. Kokonyei, G, Felvinczi, K, & Oláh, A. (2012). The development of the Problematic Online Gaming Questionnaire (POGQ).

PLoS ONE, 7(5): e36417. doi:10.1371/journal.pone. 0036417.

Griffiths, M. D. (2000). Internet addiction – Time to be taken seriously? *Addiction Research*, *8*, 413-418.

Griffiths, M. D. (2005a). A 'components' model of addiction within a biopsychosocial framework. *Journal of Substance Use*, *10*(4), 191-197.

Griffiths, M.D., King, D.L. & Demetrovics, Z. (2014). DSM-5 Internet Gaming Disorder needs a unified approach to assessment. *Neuropsychiatry*, 4(1), 1-4.

Griffiths, M.D., Kuss, D.J. & King, D.L. (2012). Video game addiction: Past, present and future. *Current Psychiatry Reviews*, 8, 308-318.

King, D.L., Delfabbro, P.H. & Griffiths, M.D. (2012). Clinical interventions for technology-based problems: Excessive Internet and video game use. *Journal of Cognitive Psychotherapy: An International Quarterly*, 26, 43-56.

King, D.L., Delfabbro, P.H., Griffiths, M.D. & Gradisar, M. (2011). Assessing clinical trials of Internet addiction treatment: A systematic review and CONSORT evaluation. *Clinical Psychology Review*, *31*, 1110-1116.

King, D.L., Delfabbro, P.H., Griffiths, M.D. & Gradisar, M. (2012). Cognitive-behavioural approaches to outpatient treatment of Internet addiction in children and adolescents. *Journal of Clinical Psychology*, *68*, 1185-1195.

King, D.L., Haagsma, M.C., Delfabbro, P.H., Gradisar, M.S. Griffiths, M.D. (2013). Toward a consensus definition of pathological video-gaming: A systematic review of psychometric assessment tools. *Clinical Psychology Review*, 33, 331-342.

Koronczai, B., Urban, R., Kokonyei, G., Paksi, B., Papp,

K., Kun, B., . . . Demetrovics, Z. (2011). Confirmation of the three-factor model of problematic internet use on off-line adolescent and adult samples. *Cyberpsychology, Behavior and Social Networking, 14*, 657–664.

Kuss, D.J. & Griffiths, M.D. (2012). Internet and gaming addiction: A systematic literature review of neuroimaging studies. *Brain Sciences, 2*, 347-374.

Pápay, O., Nagygyörgy, K., Griffiths, M.D. & Demetrovics, Z. (2014). Problematic online gaming. In K. Rosenberg & L. Feder (Eds.), *Behavioral Addictions: Criteria, Evidence and Treatment* (pp.61-95). New York: Elsevier.

Petry, N.M., & O'Brien, C.P. (2013). Internet gaming disorder and the DSM-5. *Addiction, 108*, 1186–1187.

Porter, G., Starcevic, V., Berle, D., & Fenech, P. (2010). Recognizing problem video game use. *The Australian and New Zealand Journal of Psychiatry, 44*, 120-128.

Young, K. S. (1998). Internet addiction: The emergence of a new clinical disorder. *Cyberpsychology and Behavior, 1*, 237-244.

CONTENTS

Introduction

It is likely that some degree of desperation has led you to read this book. You may have found yourself and others driven to distraction by someone else's unstoppable commitment to their gaming device. Perhaps you yourself feel enslaved to digital gaming and are looking for some guidance out of an increasingly pixelated life. It is my hope and aim that your experience at the other side of this book is one of greater knowledge and confidence in overcoming either addicted or problematic video gaming.

For the loved ones and parents of addicted gamers, I would view this book as a window into the mind of the gamer: one through which you can begin to repair the broken connections within your household. For those of you who recognise that you play games to the detriment of your lives, I would see this book as a companion as you uncover and attend to the thoughts and desires buried beneath the gaming; this is an approach that aims to preserve and value your hobby, whilst preventing it from swallowing your world.

The threat that video gaming poses to our society has more to do with how frequently it occurs than how damaging it can be. With over 30 million people in the U.K. playing video games (Internet Advertising Bureau 2011) and, at a *conservative* estimate, 3 percent of those people playing to addictive levels (C. Ferguson 2011), the problem is considerably widespread. These somewhat restrained numbers would mean that around a million people in the U.K. alone are potentially playing in an unhealthy way.

The social problems associated with gaming have all come about in roughly the last 30 years and are evolving fast. While much of our healthcare system is beginning to come to terms with the prevalence of video game addiction, the gaming industry itself is morphing rapidly, offering new ways for people to become hooked. If you think that all addicted gamers are teenaged boys, then your perception is perhaps already dated.

To be addicted to gaming is to feel as if any time spent not gaming is somehow redundant. Conversely, all time spent gaming is either wildly exciting or, far more frequently, strangely empty. Life outside of playing recedes into being a background frustration – an obstacle to gaming – having to stop and eat is irritating, getting time off sick is a windfall and having your partner insist that you spend time with them does little other than irritate or enrage you.

The most painful casualties are nearly always the gamer's immediate, personal relationships. Those who know and love someone who has become addicted will experience an alienation from the gamer; as the devices begin to dominate, the relationship becomes increasingly estranged. Usually someone in the household will try to intervene, attempting to control or limit the gaming. Parents and partners who have done so are often shocked, sometimes even frightened, by the explosive and even violent responses they are suddenly faced with; simply pulling the plug on a games console might send the gamer into an unrecognisable rage. As someone sinks deeper into gaming addiction they drift further and further from those that love them. As one addict described:

> *"Gaming became more important than my business succeeding. Gaming became more important than my children's welfare. I had somehow got to the point of not wanting anything out of life other than to play that game. That's the problem with being addicted to gaming... it becomes the most dominating thing in our lives while everything else falls apart around us."*

During seminars I have run with gamers, the most powerful indicator of there being a problem is the frequency with which they argue with their loved ones about how much they game. If they are unfortunate, they will be left: spouses will file for divorce, children will become estranged and parents will settle for their child being hidden away in their room for years on end.

The good news is that gaming addiction does not, it would seem, last. The evidence for this is, as we will discuss later, thin on the ground, but importantly, there is nothing to tell us that video gaming addiction is a life sentence. However, the nature of gaming is such that it is inherently an experience without intimacy. As a result, the risk for addicted gamers is a great loss of their close relationships before they are able to recover. When the controller is finally brought under control, who will be left?

This text provides a way of understanding the concepts of video game addiction, one which is heavily informed by my work as a psychotherapist as well as my own experiences of playing and designing video games. As a result, I write from a pro-game perspective; I do not want to write off the hobby as being fundamentally negative, but rather want to cherish what it has to offer and allow that to be enjoyed in a healthy way. I avoid describing games as inherently negative or pointless as I believe that this position alienates gamers who need help, forcing them to choose between their health and their hobby. In nearly all cases a middle road of balanced, mindful play can be found.

The first chapter will provide a realistic view of how damaging video game addiction can be, considering the worst case scenarios as well as more common outcomes.

Chapter two will look at how to recognise video game addiction by describing the most frequent and identifiable symptoms.

Chapter three takes us through some of the suggested causes of the condition, briefly considering ideas such as addiction being a disease, the addictive personality and how games themselves might be responsible. This section concludes by looking at the environmental factors that can lead people to hide away in compulsive gaming.

Chapter four is a pragmatic guide for the reader to respond to and resolve video game addiction. This section, while aimed at all readers, contains three additional sections at the end that provide more targeted advice for those suffering from addiction themselves, those that know such a person and finally mental health professionals that are working with the condition.

Gaming and addiction are huge concepts, and ones that this book seeks to explore in some depth. At the same time, the goal is to make sure that the more practical information is made more immediate. Consequently there will be two types of call-out box that appear throughout the text. These are generally not central to the book, but may well be of interest and relevance to certain readers. The first type will be **discussions** – these will generally expose areas of thinking that are controversial or philosophical, providing a springboard for those readers who want to understand or question the issues on a higher or more abstract level. The second type will be **definitions** – these will be explanations of a term that might, for some readers, be unknown, conversely allowing readers who are unfamiliar with some of the ideas to establish a more practical understanding.

Throughout the book, I talk about the gamer as a nebulous, gender-neutral third-party. This generalised language feels like the clearest way to approach the issue – by addressing the part of the person that is, to varying degrees and shades, dedicating time to video games. Certainly not everything in this book will apply to any one gamer, and each and every gamer will buck the trends talked about here in some way.

My Background

My involvement with video game addiction is considerably varied. It includes working with addicts themselves, a background as a video game designer and, perhaps most importantly, being someone who grew up immersed in gaming.

As a psychotherapist, I have been in practice nearly 10 years at the time of writing this book. Part of the shifting landscape of my work is that, increasingly, clients' lives are being experienced digitally, either through time spent on social media, browsing the internet, or playing video games. I offer a focus on this as part of my niche as a mental health practitioner. I offer support to clients who view much of their world, for better or worse, on a screen.

Quite organically I have found many of these clients to be struggling with their gaming habits and, as a result, I formed a specific method for approaching and tackling this issue, much of which this book seeks to outline.

I will confess that I originally balked at the idea of writing this book. While I spend much of my life suited-up in the role of the ever-so-serious therapist, I also spend much of the rest of my life as a self-identified hardcore gamer – someone who worked for nearly four years as a games designer and who considers themselves to be extremely pro-gaming. A great deal of the time I was training as a psychotherapist, I was surrounded by people talking with bemusement and condescension about their clients' gaming habits; the last thing I wanted to do was to add to what I saw as the already numerous voices eager to speak out against gaming.

A colleague, who works with many students that game to problematic levels, suggested I take on the issue. He argued that I would have a unique perspective. Although I disagreed, I did go out and begin to read the literature on the subject. What I quickly noticed was that much of what was out there was heavily set against video games. Frequently books will, both knowingly and inadvertently, treat games as the enemy. The result of this perspective being that you are either one of the people that is able to game without any problem, or someone who is addicted who should never go near a game again. This has the twofold effect of scaring off addicts for fear that they might lose their precious hobby, while offering no help for those who could, without being viewed as addicts, benefit from a more balanced and considered pattern of play.

This led me to the realisation that writing a book on

gaming addiction was *absolutely* what I should do. I realised that I was in a strong position to comment: I could write a book about video game addiction that promoted gaming in a positive and affirmative light. I would present the first non-wrist-slapping guide to avoiding the pitfalls of harmful gaming.

Of the problematic and addicted gamers I have worked with, some of them have wanted the problem fixed, some of them have guarded their problem fiercely, and some did not see a problem. All of them have contributed to my understanding of the issue, as have other clients I have seen, many of whom have turned toward compulsion in order to manage the distress within their lives. The quotes from gamers I have used within this text have all derived from problematic and addicted gamers that I have either counselled or interviewed – each one adapted enough to preserve their anonymity. I am very grateful for everything they have given me in understanding the problem.

I see this book as being about helping people to get the most out of their hobby of video gaming, not the least. At the core of this book is a message that I would want gamers to hear: in overusing gaming, in making it stand in for what life lacks, you are doing gaming, yourself and those you love a disservice. Gaming is hugely enjoyable when it's done with fun and abandon, but its soul is stolen away once it starts to be used to compensate for or distract from the world outside.

My Experiences as a Gamer
I have struggled to control how much I game through many periods of my life. Learning about how gaming addiction has affected others has often made me reflect

on my own tussles. Over the years things have evened out for me, as they do for many problematic gamers. I would say that I now exist on a slow moving tide that moves between being highly engaged in games in a positive way, to relying on them to drown out other difficulties by playing unhealthily, before pulling back into a period of playing very little. Some time after completing these stages I will find a game I love, pick it up and soon be once again engaged. The process does not always move in strict order, and no longer do things reach a level that impacts on my functioning. I have become very conscious of the signs and know when to and how to exercise control.

I have been keen on gaming since I was a boy. I remember at 17 years old, shortly after having bought "Final Fantasy VII", my mother asked me if I would be, 'alright for a week on [my] own in the house' while she went on holiday with her partner. I told her with considerable confidence that I would be.

I think at one point during that week I clocked 19 hours straight on my Playstation, minus a few frantic breaks when I was finally overwhelmed by the demands of my digestive tract. At the same time, when friends got in touch during that week, I would happily up and see them, with no negative feelings about leaving the game other than an excitement for when I returned. I look back on this as a period of happy and positive gaming.

This contrasts starkly with a period of ill health in my early twenties when I threw myself into playing another game in the same franchise – "Final Fantasy X-2" – to the extent that I started to lose confidence in most of my relationships. That was, on reflection, unhealthy and could have been handled differently; I don't think I ever played for 19 hours, but the ease with which I was prepared to sideline the appeals of others was clearly wrong. For months my sole housemate would carry out her life behind me, barely noticed. Nobody should have to endure such brazen indifference within their own home.

The real difference between these two experiences was that the first was driven by a genuine love of the game I was playing, while the second was a sullen alternative to a situation that I didn't want to face. Curiously and importantly, "Final Fantasy VII" was a wonderful game, one I remember fondly. "Final Fantasy X-2" was, in my opinion, a plodding rehash of things I'd seen before though it still provided a suitably numbing and lengthy series of goals that diverted my thoughts away from my life.

There is an important distinction here that is central to this book; one period of play was engaged and passionate, the other was escapist and deadening. When I have played games in an unhealthy way I have found that time spent *not* gaming has felt like wasted time. I became fixated on my in-game goals; everything else became a distraction. The more time I crammed in, the more I would obsess about making my life as efficient as possible in order to obtain the best results in the game.

These days I consider myself to be an exceptionally capable scheduler – well able to plan, account for time, finish on time and so on and so forth. Bizarrely, I would say that I learned most of this through over-gaming. Constantly, I would try to minimize all other activity in my life in create as much time as possible for gaming. I might have chores, homework and sometimes work with my father to be done, all of which I would rattle through at breakneck speed so that I could get back to my beloved ZX Spectrum, my Amiga 500, my Playstation (or Playstation 2) and more recently my Xbox 360. For those of you up to speed with gaming, you would be right to notice that I am behind the times. While being able to organise my time is clearly useful, the mindset that it sprang from was less than healthy; I needed to get my life out of my way so I could get back to gaming.

As an adult, I am aware that I still have the capacity to game problematically and I can see clearly how this hurts me. Now I know to break off a long stint of gaming some 20 minutes or so before I have to socialise or be with my family. If I don't, then the irritation of having to leave whichever virtual world I'm in the process of saving will be vented onto those around me in caustic comments and acidic ripostes. I know to avoid gaming for more than a few hours in a day, even when on holiday and on top of my responsibilities. If I game longer than this, it becomes an empty, treadmill-like experience that will leave me in a foggy haze for the little of what remains of the day.

While I love gaming, I appreciate its potential to negatively impact my mood and make others around me feel unimportant. As a psychotherapist working with many people for whom gaming is a central part of their lives, I see this awareness and experience as an asset of mine. I know the struggle – to some small extent I'm still working through it.

The Appeal of Video Games

In order to be able to work with any addiction, it is important to find a way to empathise with the appeal of the behaviour. With gaming, this means understanding the fundamental appeal of games and discovering the particular nature of them that draws people to take part in the first place. Being both a gamer and someone that has created games for a living, this is a subject that has fascinated me for years and tells me a lot about what it is to be human.

The gaming industry has grown from nothing to a majority pastime in less than 50 years: a relative blink of an eye. There are many parents and mental health professionals that managed to get through an entire childhood without playing a single digital game. For such people, it is a huge but by no means impossible leap of empathy to understand how 'young' people today can commit whole days to running around virtual worlds or find themselves packing every spare minute with repeated check-ins on their non-existent kingdoms.

Even for those that are deeply immersed in the hobby, it might be hard to capture what draws people to dedicate such vast amounts of their precious time. What follows is an outline of the core appeals of gaming, as it is understood within the industry itself. The bedrock for this comes from the work of Richard Bartle (Bartle 2009), who developed the Bartle Test of Internet Gaming. While Bartle's ideas are broadly considered dated within the world of game development, they nonetheless form the foundation of how the business has come to recognize what players look for in games:

Socializing: The internet has opened up endless possibilities for meeting up with others in order to play video games. This has proved to have colossal importance for gamers. Much of the reason for this comes from our basic desire to be with others. Games can enhance this by allowing players to assist, gift and form guilds with one another, making their friendships tangible and measurable. An example of a game which relies heavily on socializing would be "Second Life".

Creativity: In games you are given characters to develop, worlds to build and cities to decorate. As a result players are able to use games as a powerful medium for both self-expression and self-exploration. This offers the chance to simultaneously engage in ultimately frivolous acts of design and creation while also enabling the deeper processing of unconscious fears and struggles. An example of a game that heavily relies upon creativity would be "Minecraft".

Accomplishment: Typically all progress made in games is clearly documented and reported though feedback. As a result, games offer a way for players to see 'constant measurable growth', allowing them to persistently explore the game with a concrete sense of improvement, something we might struggle to find in the outside world. As a result, the surmountable difficulty that games provide is an immense proportion of their appeal. An example of a game that heavily relies upon accomplishment would be "The Legend of Zelda".

Competition: Video games offer us a pure and safe way through which to gain superiority over others. Games that pitch us head-to-head come with the inherent excitement and fear of proving ourselves relative to someone else. Once again, this aspect of games has been greatly enhanced through the connectivity of the internet, which enables worldwide competitions and leagues to be accessible from our bedrooms. An example of a game that relies heavily upon competition would be "Tekken".

Immersion: Out of all of these aspects of gaming, this is the one that is perhaps the most unique to video gaming. The others could be attributed to many games that existed thousands of years before the first computer, but digital games allow us to become immersed to a powerful new level. Whole worlds and histories can be explored and interacted with. Players are able to exist through alter-egos in environments that look and sound increasingly real, and where the narratives are becoming ever more compelling. An example of a game that heavily relies upon immersion would be "The Elder Scrolls Online".

While video gaming has brought together these appeals in new and concentrated forms, they are all sources of enjoyment that we can understand on a broad, historic and human level. Where a child might turn to "The Elder Scrolls" to become immersed today, they might have used a novel a century ago. Where an adult might prove themselves in a game of "Fifa", they might have once opted for an actual game of football.

A difference between these more time-honoured pastimes and video gaming is that the latter frequently ends up being played addictively. Whether, for any given individual, this propensity to addiction might have expressed itself in the absence of games remains unknown; as a society we have seen the power of video games to become addictive and we are, as a whole, concerned.

Discussion: The Fear of the New
Much accessible literature on the subject of gaming addiction presents the picture of a digital plague that is

sweeping through our younger generations via modems. In 2010 the BBC ran a "Panorama" episode on the subject, arguably presenting games as a genuine danger to our youth. This is, admittedly, far sexier and news-worthy than the reality whereby, out of those people that game regularly, at least 9 out of 10 of them will do so with no adverse effects (Gentile et al 2009). Furthermore, what studies have been carried out imply that gaming addiction will tend to naturally resolve itself (King 2013a) with no lasting effects.

In more recent years, both The Sun and The Daily Mail have carried out articles that have compared gaming addiction to alcohol and hard drugs (Pafitt 2014). The former headline, in 2014, stated, 'Gaming as addictive as heroin'. Not only are the bold claims made very questionable, they also run the risk, in my opinion, of alienating addicted gamers from getting help. If we are to exaggerate the dangers of gaming, we will not be taken seriously by those suffering from gaming addiction.

Historically, society has had a tendency to exaggerate the dangers of new technologies. Socrates decried the invention of writing, declaring that it would 'create forgetfulness in the learners' souls', and that people would 'appear to be omniscient and will generally know nothing' (Plato). Current fears about new technology are not limited to video gaming. As social media, the internet and mobile devices are all continuing their inexorable march toward the forefront of our lives, alarmist concerns for our mental wellbeing follow close behind. This is no surprise. Bad news sells – we are hardwired to prioritise being vigilant for things that might hurt us. Given a choice between a positive article and an article that contains a scare, we are almost always going to be more interested in the latter.

The historian Melvin Kranzberg rightly pointed out in his first law of technology that, "Technology is neither good nor bad; nor is it neutral" (Kranzberg 1986). To argue for games being a 'bad' or even a 'good' thing is to take part in a futile and never-ending debate. We are best off accepting the presence and importance of new technologies before establishing how best to make use of them.

The Evolution of Video Game Addiction

It is not enough for us to simply accept that some people will become addicted to games, regardless of the games themselves. There is plenty of evidence, both anecdotal and based in research that tells us that certain games lead to harmful play more than others. The absolute top suspect routinely comes out as being MMOs (see below for a definition). "Everquest", one of the first and biggest such game, became widely known as 'Evercrack'. Similarly "World of Warcraft" has, unfairly or fairly, earned itself the nickname of 'World of Warcrack'. These references to the hardest of hard drugs go a long way to revealing the effect that games of this genre have had on users. Research has shown that the second and third gaming genres most likely to induce excessive play are FPSs and RTSs respectively (Nagygyörgy 2013). All of the above gaming types are largely popular due to their social and/or competitive nature – something that was enhanced dramatically with the advent of the internet. Today gaming is changing again, and with it the nature of gaming addiction.

A Brief Guide to Gaming Genres

Massively Multiplayer Online Roleplaying Game (MMORPG or MMO)

These include the likes of "World of Warcraft", "Eve Online" and "Guild Wars". All such games rely upon huge open worlds in which you can engage in a near endless series of quests that constantly progress you while simultaneously linking you to a wide network of other gamers. Research and common opinion agree that this type of game is by far the most prone to being used addictively.

First Person Shooter (FPS)

One of the more addictive gaming genres, though not as addictive as the MMORPG, these games involve a character-eye view down the barrel of a gun. They typically offer a lengthy single-player game (one that can be enjoyed alone) and a very deep range of competitive, online game modes. Games of this genre would include "Call of Duty", "Battlefield" and "Killzone".

Roleplaying (RPG)

Named after the dungeon-crawling pen and paper game "Dungeons and Dragons", this genre has grown to encompass any game that involves a levelling system (whereby your character gets more powerful with their successes) and a sense of being immersed in a fantasy setting. In contrast to MMORPGs games such as this are more story-focused and can generally only be played alone. Games of this genre would include "Final Fantasy", "Skyrim" and "Dark Souls". As with MMORPGs, these games are all known for their relative complexity and the commitment required from gamers in order to be enjoyed fully.

Real Time Strategy (RTS)

Another gaming genre that is prone toward being played addictively, the real time strategy game involves staging a battle with either a squad of men or a vast army, typically viewed from an aerial perspective. Real Time Strategies are highly competitive games that are frequently played against other players online. "Starcraft, Empire: Total War" and "Company of Heroes" are typical RTSs.

Match Three

The only exclusively 'casual' genre in the list. These games involve moving objects round on a board in an attempt to create lines of three that share the same colour. Match Three games are pleasingly intuitive to play and tend to create dazzling effects and cascades with relatively little skill on the player's behalf. "Candy Crush Saga", "Bejewelled Blitz" and "Fluffy Birds Flash" are examples of Match Three games.

Multi-player Online Battle Arena (MOBA)

Increasingly popular in recent years, the MOBA is an online team-based game against another team of online players in which both sides try to fight past each other to reach opposing objectives. MOBA games and their communities are highly competitive environments. Examples of this genre would be "League of Legends" and "DOTA 2".

While video game addiction may be nearly as old as video games, the ways in which it is commonly understood inevitably lag someway behind. This is largely because of the baffling speed at which video games are evolving. "XCOM: Enemy Unknown", which was released in 2012, provides a powerful description of this evolution. The game was a remake of the original "UFO: Enemy Unknown" from 1994; they had taken an old title and updated it with the latest in both graphics and game design. The difference between the two versions is a startling testament to how far the industry has progressed. The '90s version was a pixilated, washed out, 2D experience from a fixed perspective. The game could only be played on a (then) powerful, home computer, requiring you to take time out to find the disk, watch it load and then commit time to it. The reboot had a fully 3D look, with each character and set brought to life with shadows and realistic animations. Additionally, the game was not only playable on home computers and consoles but also on a portable tablet. The new "XCOM" was a radically more visually immersive game that you could quickly enjoy on the bus to work in the morning, a vastly different experience from the original. As fast as we become accustomed to video games within our world, the reality of their relationship with us advances at a far quicker rate.

These kinds of improvements to technology haven't necessarily led to better games, as any old-school, mid-thirties gamer will no doubt vehemently tell you, but it has led to a startling increase in the level of immersion of which modern games are capable. "Red Dead Redemption", the 2010 award-winning game from Rockstar, was testament to the immersive power of recent games. The cowboy simulator brought the Wild West to life with sweeping vistas from the border of Mexico, wind that softly howls and picks up dust and foliage around you and all manner of wildlife scurrying to and fro as you pound your horse across the dusty plains. It is difficult to play this game for more than a few minutes and not be swept into its world.

Up until about 10 years ago, the games industry was increasingly dominated by games such as this, known as Triple A games – the blockbusters of gaming. These titles had big names behind them, required vast teams and vast amounts of money to make and were then pushed out for a one time charge of £40/$60. This business model capitalised on the presence of consoles and gaming-capable PCs being in nearly everyone's home – a far cry from the early '90s and '80s when most gamers would need to hang out at their local arcade with a pocket full of change to play anything half-decent.

Definition: Triple A Title

Triple A denotes a top of the range game that has been released as a purchasable product (often a boxed product) at a high price point (£40 in the U.K. or $60 in the U.S.). Triple A is historically the best of the best in video gaming and was where the industry saw most of its revenue. Recent developments in freemium games have seen a gradual shift in this area, however. Triple A games are by definition only made by extremely large and wealthy studios. "Call of Duty: Black Ops", "GTA V" and "Final Fantasy XIII" are examples of Triple A titles.

A large portion of the public's perception of video gaming and video game addiction is stuck around this period. The gamer is still seen by many as the sickly, single, male youth hunched over a console. Public opinion on video gaming is neatly captured by Warner Brothers' "The Big Bang Theory". This sitcom describes the plight of three young(ish) socially inept and far from Adonis-like males, all of whom are slavishly hooked on geek culture in all its forms, video games being no exception. Interestingly, the series explores gaming addiction by having Penny, the great looking blonde from across the hall, discover MMOs only to sink into a compulsive pit of greasy hair, burger-stuffing and sullen ugliness. The episode's joke goes a long way to expose perceptions of the addicted gamer. How could a good-looking woman with common sense ever end up addicted to video games?

While the perceived image of addicts as awkward young men still bears some relation to the majority of addicts, the market has changed dramatically in the last 15 years. The nature and accessibility of games today has opened up a new wealth of consumers who use games in a whole new range of ways, many of these being less than healthy. I saw one lady in her 40s who struggled to control how much she played on her mobile phone. This individual by no means fit the stereotypical description of the gaming addict, yet she described the game as having 'taken away [her] self-control'. She depicted herself as wanting to:

> *"...play it at any opportunity I had, any time I had a spare minute, and sometimes even when I didn't. When my friends pointed out that I was playing it in a pub during a night out I realised that things had gone very wrong."*

These developments in gaming have new kinds of gamers; some of them are addicted in new ways. We are, as ever, struggling to catch up with the changes.

"Flappy Bird" is perhaps one of the games that most powerfully accentuates this enormous shift in how gaming technology is being used. Ten years ago it would be hard to believe that within a decade, a single, unknown independent developer in Vietnam would end up pulling his solo project from the market because he was concerned that his game, bringing in $50,000 a *day*, was proving *too addictive*. Compare a game such as "Flappy Bird" to a Triple A game such as "The Last of Us", a game released in the same year with armies of staff, years of production and whose background code dwarfs that of "Flappy Bird" thousands of times over. There is clearly a colossal gulf between the production standard of these titles and yet these smaller, infinitely cheaper games are weighing in with heavyweight profits. While "The Last of Us" was a profitable game, many Triple A studios, such as THQ, that were flourishing some 10 years ago, have now disappeared. The market has greatly diversified to benefit the new wave of 'casual' games, taking much of the power away from the former giants of the industry and drastically changing who games and how they game.

This is all hardly surprising. "Flappy Bird" made a lot of money but its income is paltry compared to the unthinkable profit of other similarly simplistic games on the market at the moment. "Candy Crush Saga" is and has been for some time, the most astonishing example of the triumph of the (comparatively) small-budget, mobile game. This game's developers – the U.K.-based King – were at one point reportedly pulling in over $3.5 million a day from a 2D game where you push sweets about. That's far over 50 times what "Flappy Bird" was doing (BGR 2014). And he thought his game was worryingly addictive. So what happened?

The Rise of Casual Gaming

Today's gaming market has split into what is loosely referred to as casual and hardcore gaming – definitions that have further sub-divided and merged into a wide plethora of different gaming styles. This has led to a diversifying in the ways that people play; changes that even the game design industry struggles to keep up with. Most notably, these changes are created by the rise of mobile gaming and the free-to-play model.

Definition: Mobile Gaming

All gaming that is carried out on a portable device. While this primarily refers to smartphones and tablets, it can also include handhelds such as the PS Vita and Nintendo 3DS. Mobile gaming offers a far higher level of access to gamers and is best suited to short bursts of play. Consequently games designed for these platforms tend to favour more frivolous, snack-able formats.

To clarify the language here: hardcore gaming is typically on a console or a PC, involves playing for several hours, sometimes days at a time, and normally centres on some kind of killing/violence/carnage in a fantasy or military setting. This is still largely the domain of men, with only around a fifth of such games being played by women (Williams 2009). Hardcore games include the likes of "Call of Duty", "Skyrim" and "Titanfall" and are, certainly historically, a realm dominated by the Triple A titles.

Casual games, on the other hand, are typically played on mobile devices or through internet browsers. These are frequently disposable, colourful games that centre on nurturing, building and decorating as well as puzzle and quiz games. "Farmville", "Clash of Clans" and "Candy Crush Saga" are all arguably examples of this broad style of game. Recent reports suggest that women have taken the lead in this market, playing marginally more than men (Sky News 2013). A telltale sign of casual gamers is that they can spend hours playing such games and still not self-identify as gamers. To them, a couple of minutes here and there pushing sweets in "Candy Crush" doesn't equate to being a gamer, even when a couple of minutes here and there totals more than a fifth of their waking hours.

Mobiles have, in an incredibly short space of time, completely changed the experience of being either in a city or on public transport. Mobile gaming forms an important part of that shift. Phones are out in force wherever you go, and a great many of those screens are busy housing some form of video game. My gamer's eye is always caught by the distinctive green expanse of someone tending to their clan in "Clash of Clans" or the ponderous swipes of a sweet pusher.

In *The Fix*, a somewhat melodramatic 'we're-all-doomed' discussion on addiction by Telegraph writer Damian Thompson, is the astute observation that a crucial ingredient for addiction is access – and phones are all about access. You can push sweets on the toilet, under the meeting table, in bed, over your lover's shoulder, even in a real sweet shop. Thompson argues that our evolutionary impulses to seek out rewarding behaviour backfire on us badly in situations where there is no limit to the supply of rewards. He cites the use of gin in 18th-century England, heroin use in Vietnam and sugary foods in modern, Western society, all instances where we are missing a natural ceiling to how much 'goodness' we can get and are subsequently going all out in getting far too much for us to handle (Thompson 2013).

By this reckoning, mobile gaming will be off the charts. As of yet, there is evidence that mobile gaming is hugely popular, but little to say that it is, as yet, proving dangerously addictive – two very different things as we will discuss later. At the same time, the reports of people sinking vast quantities of money and time into seemingly cute and innocuous mobile games are slowly trickling in to form a new, bigger picture of gaming addiction (Rogers 2014).

There are a couple of developments in the world of mobile gaming that are particularly cruel in their appeal to potential addicts, namely appointment gameplay and the free-to-play business model. Both of these are already eliciting vast amounts of time and cash from the public and, given the propensity for video games to become the object of addiction, it is important that we make ourselves aware of the potential that this more recent form of gaming has to consume our lives.

Appointment Gameplay

Casual (and thereby most mobile) games typically follow the appointment model of gameplay. This simply means that there is a real-time delay between the action and the reward, the classic example from "Farmville" being that once you have planted your seeds (action), you need to wait a few minutes, sometimes a few hours, before you are able to return and harvest your crops (reward). This style of gameplay is prolific on mobiles and sets up gamers for a new and accessible trap within which they can find themselves addicted.

As with most successful games, the appointment

system is anything but 'instant gratification'. In fact, it is, by design, the opposite. I've noticed that you can often spot an academic, non-gamer talking about games by their frequent references to concepts such as 'instant gratification' and 'constant rewards' – it doesn't take long playing any successful game (beyond the tutorials which are always full of rewards) to realise that games, certainly at a more dedicated level, are predominantly about failure and denial (Juul 2013). In appointment-based games you are forced to wait; playing "Clash of Clans" I frequently had to wait days, sometimes even weeks for certain rewards to filter through. In addition, you are regularly denied the option to continue playing after you have performed a certain number of other actions, ranging from laughably trivial to downright invasively difficult.

Many people I encountered in the world of game design hate the appointment gaming model with a passion, seeing it as the anathema of good gaming. Much of the hatred is that this withdrawal of gameplay from the user is seen as a move solely designed to force people into choosing between paying and waiting. In my opinion and experience, this model of design is inherently attractive to a certain type of player. Whether there is a payment scheme or not, they are going find considerable enjoyment in this system.

Because appointment dynamics work around brief periods of gameplay followed by longer periods of waiting, it makes an excellent fit with mobile players. When I was designing these types of games our audience was primarily seen to be female, Japanese commuters in their late 30s and early 40s. This demographic was considered to be spending much of their time either travelling through urban environments or working hard in high-powered, demanding and/or oppressive jobs. Appointment gaming on their mobile phones offered them a way to turn the hiatuses in their day into colourful, rewarding bursts of gaming. The knock-on effect being that they could spend the next stretch of work/travelling/meetings covertly looking forward to their next 'visit' to the game when they could pick up their rewards. They might feed their baby cow before an important meeting, knowing that by the time said meeting had ended, they could check in to see it fully grown and rewarding them with a pail of milk.

This is a stark example of a form of gameplay that is becoming increasingly common, particularly with the rise of always-on, always-connected portable devices such as tablets and smart phones. Increasingly we are offered a way to fill in 'gaps' in our day. Every aspect of phones and tablets is designed to create a sense of attachment and pleasure in the user, leading to the simple act of holding and checking the phone acting as a comforting and rewarding act in itself (Thompson 2013). Not only this, but due to the widely accepted behaviour of looking at one's phone more than one's surroundings, it is relatively easy to wrap many hours of this type of gameplay into a working day without anyone ever even knowing that you're doing so, including you. This goes some way to explaining the infrequency with which such casual gamers see themselves as being gamers. All in all, appointment gameplay, especially on mobiles, is an increasingly ripe source of addiction.

Historically, the days of shelling out £40 – £50 on a single, complete game and then going off and enjoying it at no further cost are diminishing. Sales figures point to an acutely sharp decline in the number of big gaming publishing houses producing Triple A titles (Robinson 2013). That said, "Grand Theft Auto V" became the fastest selling game of all time in 2013 and the end of the previous year saw the release of Sony and Microsoft's next generation of consoles, so we can safely say that we will continue to see this sales model over the next few years, at least.

From the wings, however, the free-to-play model has blossomed, initially being a hit on mobiles and social networks, and now being increasingly popular on PCs. Free-to-play games are, shockingly, actually free-to-play, with additional features, resources, power-ups and customization available to all gamers… provided they are prepared to pay. Typically these virtual goods will be inexpensive and transient; you pay a seemingly insignificant amount of money, get a temporary boost that you can use once or twice in the game and then it's gone. A common combination is to offer a free-to-play game with an appointment system, such that players are frequently asked to wait in order to progress, but have the option to pay in order to speed things along. Some powerful examples of current free-to-play games are "Candy Crush Saga" (whose otherworldly revenue we have already mentioned), "Planetside 2" and "World of Tanks".

Free-to-play relies partly upon a small number of users making frequent, minimal purchases. More importantly, it relies upon an even smaller number of users, termed 'whales', sinking an inordinate amount of money into virtual goods. It is widely understood that in order to make a game such as this profitable, there needs to be an infinite number of huge purchases that a minority of gamers can make without them running out of content to play through. This is typically achieved by pitching said gamers against one another, culminating in an arms race where, arguably, only the developers are victorious. "Clash of Clans" is an excellent example of a game that uses this model, with some users dropping literally thousands of dollars a month into the game (Rigney 2012).

The sinister undertone of the free-to-play business model is that it potentially depends upon pathological or addictive gaming in order to reach financial success. This is a growing concern, particularly in Japan, where they have begun to create laws to catch some of what they consider to be more devious mechanics within free-to-play games. Increasingly, attention is drawn to the huge amounts of money that users can easily pump into these games. For many players, this is a potential criterion for addiction – increasing numbers of gamers are finding that their need to compensate for what is missing in their lives through their gaming is now resulting in a hefty financial cost, much like pathological gambling.

These new forms of gaming, appointment and free-to-play, are arguably not problematic in themselves, much the same as hardcore gaming. Someone stealing several hours of their day to play "Clash of Clans" on their tablet is not a problem, per se, and we need to be aware that the bulk of the existing (although potentially outdated) research out there points the finger at the young male playing online hardcore games as the most frequent of the video game addicts. However, if that person fails to pick up their daughter because they need to raid that last bit of gold, or finds themselves unable to heat their house because they have spent increasingly more on virtual gems to grow their clan, then there is a serious issue that needs resolving. For those few that can't control the way they interact with these new forms of gaming, they will need to address their lifestyle just as any hardcore gamer would.

Is This Just About Men?

While it is less and less the case that gaming is a male only pastime, boys that game to addicted levels still outnumber the equivalent girls by a whopping 50 percent (Gentile et al 2009). This forms part of a wider picture described by thinkers such as Sax and Zimbardo who believe there to be a large-scale disillusionment in the young men of today; both these writers consider video games to be one of the core reasons for this.

Games are still largely made *by* men *for* men. Women still feature relatively scarcely in game design teams. I remember a woman joining our team after about a year of my working as a game designer in Brighton. This particular artist was, by virtue of her gender, a novelty. If one is to discount certain, more female-populated roles such as art, HR and marketing teams, you are left with programming and design, two areas of the industry that are almost entirely populated by men. Exceptions exist, such as Robin Hunicke of "The Sims", but these roles are nearly all taken up by males, a situation that is, gradually and thankfully, changing. As a result of the gender skew in development, there is a bias toward games fulfilling exclusively male fantasies, which explains the dominance of action and violence in hardcore gaming.

There is a further concern that the lack of male role models for young men has caused their mass flight into gaming. As the character of Tyler Durden said in "Fight Club", "We are a generation of men raised by women, the last thing we need is another woman" (though that was all the way back in the '90s). Is it the case that many guys grow up without having a clear sense of how to be a man? Robert Bly in *Iron John* poetically tells us that 'soft' men today have lost touch with the sense of the primitive 'wild man'. He describes the few fathers that are present in households as being bumbling fools in the background (Bly 1990) – an image that is repeated time and time again in primetime sitcoms ("The Simpsons", "Malcolm in the Middle", "Modern Family", "My Family"). Zimbardo certainly links this to gaming addiction, saying that "guys become confused about what acceptable male behaviour is" and find themselves, post feminism, struggling to direct the violent fantasies that naturally occur for them (Zimbardo 2012). The hack and slash of video games, in Zimbardo's opinion, offer an outlet for these feelings and become all consuming.

Games offer a primarily male nirvana – a playground of violence and heroics that has no tangible consequences. Being young has, over the centuries, probably become harder as much as it has become easier, but the ways in which we are able to manage and cope with this have changed dramatically. For boys, the classic hardcore form of gaming is a tailor-made outlet. For women the gaming industry is quickly developing to catch up with their interests. As a result it is prudent to consider video game addiction as being a pan-gender issue.

CHAPTER ONE

The Damage of Video Game Addiction

Nearly every day there are new articles published about video game addiction. These range from the mildly concerned to the outright scare-mongering. It is very difficult to know exactly what is at risk when a gamer plays too much, or more importantly, plays to the point of becoming addicted. This chapter seeks to bring together some of the evidence and give a realistic overview of the short and long-term risks of someone being addicted to video games.

Gaming addiction, at its most severe, can have a harmful effect on a person's wellbeing. While there are a range of ways in which this can happen, the damage is most acute in how it affects a person's relationship with others. It can limit confidence in social interactions as well as creating tension, alienation and conflict within a household.

There is relatively little physical risk associated with gaming too much; typically what harm is done to the body is minimal and only affects a small percentage of addicted gamers. Symptoms that do occur include: insomnia, poor attention span, motion sickness, headaches, dry eyes, muscle pains, various repetitive strain injuries, and auditory hallucinations. All of the above conditions will typically pass once the gamer ceases to game so frequently (King 2013b). There are instances where gaming has been linked to epilepsy. This is something that the gaming industry has had to address in the way it uses light and animation; both "Pokémon" and "Super Mario" having to be redesigned following some adverse responses from users. Overall, while the chance of a seizure does increase for gamers, the likelihood of it happening is considerably less than a percent of a percent (CSPH 2007). If anything it is a useful incentive to make sure gaming doesn't go on in isolation – something I'll talk more about later.

When it comes to the physical dangers of gaming, the most pressing issue is the *general* lack of health that we end up with once we spend long periods of time sitting still. A shortage of exercise, a typically poor sitting position and no time in the fresh air and sun is well documented as having general negative impact on physical and mental health. But our bodies are not where we should prioritise our concerns; it is too often relationships that are the real casualty of video game addiction.

The Social Risk of Gaming

An addiction to gaming will almost certainly create a number of significant social problems; ultimately becoming a catch-22, like any other addiction. Whatever the problems were that drove a person to overuse gaming, those problems will start to magnify once the behaviour becomes addictive. This can lead the gamer to turn to gaming even more in order to feel better, and so the problems spiral until the gamer finally and decisively changes course.

Unless steps are taken to reduce gaming addiction,

sufferers will ultimately see their relationships wither away, possibly even becoming irreparably lost. There will be those that will simply stop wasting their time trying to get in touch or arranging to meet. Loved ones will, if the gamer is lucky, start to fight back against the games, insisting upon time being put back into themselves and others. If the gamer is not so lucky then they will gradually see even these relationships fall away. This will happen slowly and subtly; it is often the case that addicted gamers fail to see the extent to which they have drifted away until they are forced to reflect on how things used to be. This damage is particularly acute for people who become addicted in their teenage years. While such people are likely to overcome the gaming addiction, they will find themselves playing social catch-up with their peers, something they may never feel like they can achieve in the long run.

The most addictive games are online roleplaying games, such as the incredibly successful "World of Warcraft", whereby players will be constantly engaging with one another online (Nagygyorgy 2013). While there is nothing unreal about the connection and bond that gamers feel with one another online, it crucially lacks the face-to-face experience that we encounter in the world away from games. Many young men I have worked with are drawn to these relationships because they find them to be more dependable and trustworthy relationships, something we will talk more about later. For now it is important to note that even though gamers may have a thriving social life online, they are often lacking an important aspect of human connection in not being with people in person – one that will gradually erode their confidence should they not redress the online/offline balance.

Online social interactions within games are frequently negative. For all the benefits of having an anonymous internet, the disadvantage is that for many people, this lack of accountability gives them permission to be negative and even insulting toward one another. For those that are new to games they will often have to stand up to ridicule at their lack of familiarity with the game, and at higher levels the competitiveness and intensity of the challenge can frequently lead to bullying, trash-talking and flaming. Many of the young people I have worked with have developed a negative worldview which, in part, I see as a direct result of their being over exposed to this cynical and hostile environment.

Definition: Trash-talking and Flaming

Both of the above are forms of negative comments made by other internet users (and in this case, gamers) toward one another. Trash-talking occurs in competitive games and is when someone deliberately insults another player in order to intimidate them into losing. Flaming (sometimes in the form of trolling) is when a player will deliberately make inflammatory remarks in order to derail situations or get a reaction.

Conflict between gamers and their significant others is a very real problem when someone becomes addicted. Most notably, this conflict occurs at the inevitable point where others try to stop or interrupt the gaming. This situation can frequently lead to addicted gamers sulking, arguing, becoming suddenly overcome with emotion and, in extreme cases, violent. Some parents have reported the horror at their typically placid teenage son suddenly attacking them when they turned off the games console.

This is an extreme example, but the extreme change in mood can be dramatic, immediate and disturbing.

Much of this is a defence mechanism. When someone has come to rely upon gaming in order to defend against the fear, pain or loss they experience in their lives they know full well that others will be looking to take their gaming away from them. Addicted gamers will, sometimes knowingly, allow their ill mood to run riot whenever the subject of limiting play is mentioned: shouting, tantrums, sulking and storming out are all viable tactics. They rely upon others prioritising an easier life of just letting them game over the more difficult and conflict-ridden life of helping them get better. At the same time, it is also important to remember that games have their natural high and low points. Stopping playing when you have completed a mission with friends is quite natural and feels right, but being ripped from a game when you are at the culmination of an hour long quest in which your friends need you most would enrage anybody. As discussed later on, it is important that people supporting games through addiction familiarize themselves with the schedules of gaming in order to rule out the natural conflict that can occur from others having an insensitivity to games.

When a gamer becomes overinvolved in gaming, the shift back to normality can create a period of unease that creates tension with others. While this is more an issue of playing excessively (playing for long periods of time) rather than addictively (playing in a way that hurts you and others), the effect is likely to be noticeable in any instance of addiction. Video games are all about immersion, both through the creation of flow in the activity (Csikszentmihalyi 2002) and the simulation of being in another world. Typically, if a gamer plays for any prolonged period, the gamer will have to readjust to the out-of-game world once he has finished. In comparison to the world within a game, the outside world has a number of striking differences.

1. **It has depth.** The gamer is required to now see and navigate things coming and going at varying distances unlike the mock 3D of the gaming world.

2. **It requires contact with the body.** The gamer, who has been little more than eyes, ears, fingers and a brain is now having to notice and control their whole body.

3. **It contains others in close proximity.** Suddenly people are right next to you, with all the confusions of body language, physical contact and expressions.

4. **You mind is free to wander.** Games require attention, thereby taking you away from other anxieties and stressors that will otherwise flood into the space left behind.

5. **You are at risk.** Games are safe environments. While your character may die, you are always able to keep restarting. The outside world offers no such assurance.

Definition: Flow

Flow is a psychological concept described by Mihaly Csikszentmihalyi. When a person engages in an activity that presents them with a level of challenge that matches their level of skill they reach a state of immersion and timelessness that is termed 'flow' (Csikszentmihalyi 2002). Basic game design involves attempting to keep the player in a state of constant flow by ensuring that the difficulty increases in gentle 'waves'.

It is during the period of adjusting between the world of the game and the world outside that gamers will often become agitated or moody. The changes in experience lead to the gamer experiencing a low-level and persistent threat, one that can create a sense of hypervigilance and anxiety.

This increased sense of threat and complexity can generate defensiveness and distraction in the gamer. This is normally present in gamers that have just stopped gaming even if they are far from being addicted; if someone plays for a prolonged session, they will likely be perceived as distant, non-responsive and sometimes mildly argumentative by others during that post-game period of adjustment. For gamers that play games addictively, this often leads to full on conflict.

Much of the above takes us into the murky waters of the links between video games and aggression. This subject is not one we can do justice to here, suffice to say that the field is littered with contradicting studies on the subject. There is, perhaps, a marginal inclination toward the possibility that they do, to a degree, have this effect (McClean 2013) if only in the short-term and not to the extent of violence. Consequently, it is worth bearing in mind that gaming has the potential to create brief, aggressive feelings in the gamer, something only likely to become profoundly noticeable where addiction is present.

Perhaps you are close to someone who is addicted to games and you recognise that you would rather avoid falling out with them rather than step in and assert that this behaviour is unacceptable. Consider this decision you are making, reflect on it and make sure you know where you stand and that you feel it is the right decision. This is particularly important for parents; I would argue that your role is not to be liked, but to do the best by your children. If they are gaming in an unhealthy way, then compassionately intervene, even if this means risking their anger.

Can Video Game Addiction Kill?

In short – no. While there are an incredibly small number of deaths that happen in relation to gaming, these tend to do little more than provide fuel for the media fire that surrounds video gaming. These unfortunate cases make for sensational reading, but don't build up into any significant picture about the lethality of gaming.

There are a number of instances whereby players have died after gaming for prolonged periods, presumably too involved in the game to attend to their physical needs, such as sleep, urination and simply moving around. At some point the body packs up and the heart gives out, finally enforcing an end to the gaming session, as well as their lives. There have been a handful of such deaths; nearly all of them, strangely, in South Korea; although Taiwan had a similar incident recently. The Korean government has subsequently taken controversial steps to limit gamers' access to online gaming, which is now shut off to under 16-year-olds past midnight.

In addition, there are a number of further instances where video games have been made accountable for murder, killings and manslaughter. These include a couple letting their baby starve to death while they were too busy feeding their online baby, a young man killing his friend over the loss of a virtual sword and a son shooting his parents while they slept. These deaths are almost incalculably rare. Exact numbers are hard to pin down but are globally estimated at around 10 in recent memory. Considering the 8,367 alcohol related deaths in the U.K. in 2012 alone (Office for National Statistics 2014), this makes gaming a comparatively very safe pastime. To talk about gaming as being lethal is to miss the point. When games do damage it is to our social and emotional lives; that is the concern that we should be focused on.

A Lack of Embodiment

A particular concern is for the gamer's sense of embodiment. This is by no means an issue localized to excessive gaming, but expands to cover computer, phone and tablet usage more generally. The education advisor Ken Robinson, during a TED video, talked of the temptation for people to "look upon their body as a form of transport for their heads" (Robinson 2006). As we move to spending more and more time connected to devices, this trap of forgetting our bodies is set to become a regular challenge for current and subsequent generations. A recent report revealed that, in the early part of 2013, every one in 12 waking minutes used by people in Britain was spent online (IAB 2013). That's a considerable portion of our time (not including television) that we are spending focused on the digital, rather than the physical world.

During time spent at computer and mobile screens, we lose a sense of being connected to our bodies. More and more, we are finding out the importance of having an experience of the wholeness of our beings; much of today's mindfulness-based psychotherapy involves encouraging people to make contact with their otherwise forgotten physical selves (Siegel 2011). All emotions are situated in the body, something that rapidly becomes apparent in psychotherapy. If you were to experience happiness and I were to ask you where in your body you felt it, then either immediately or after some reflection, you would more likely be able to describe the physical sensation as well as the exact place in your body where you felt it. Most likely it would be a fullness in your chest, but it could also be a buzzing in your stomach or a lightness in your limbs. Other emotions are the same; all of them manifest physically. Our emotional weather is not something that goes on within just our minds or even our brains, but runs throughout our whole system. Your stomach churns when you panic, your heart leaps in love, your brow sweats in fear, and so on and so on.

For gamers who find themselves addicted, time spent online is time spent largely shut off from their emotional being; they have effectively blinkered themselves from themselves. The result of this is that they come to be so disconnected by their feelings (feelings that they inevitably experience whenever they are away from the game) that they become distrustful and almost scornful toward them, as if they are something to be repressed, fought against and sedated. Ultimately, this puts people at odds with themselves, leading to a deep existential unease, one that is further expressed by their increasing fear of time spent away from gaming. For such people the most obvious way to deal with this is more gaming.

Definition: Existential
This word refers to anything that is to do with the fundamentals of our existence. Typical existential concerns are death, being isolated from others, having to make meaning out of a meaningless world, not having any freedom and conversely having too much freedom such

that we are overwhelmed by choice. We all struggle with existential problems at some level and can react strongly to situations when we perceive an existential threat. Existentialism is chiefly ascribed to the works of Jean-Paul Sartre and Martin Heidegger.

How Gaming Addiction Hurts Gaming

Gaming is a wonderful hobby: it demonstrates mind-blowing technology, is a huge source of fun and energy between friends and offers us a myriad of alternative worlds to enjoy. Any addictive use will not only hurt the gamer but also the act of gaming itself. Addicted gamers know this all too well. They will fight back against any acknowledgement or treatment of the issue, knowing that should they give in, they will need to seriously review their habits, possibly even stopping gaming altogether. On a number of other levels, the process of becoming addicted seriously compromises the act of playing; regularly turning what should be fun into something that is poisonous, guilt-ridden and even laborious.

Frequently, addicted gamers will become aware of the negativity created by their obsession and begin to engage in the 'binge-purge cycle', a concept commonly associated with eating disorders. Players will find themselves disliking their games and their gaming, but will nonetheless remain compelled to continue using them. Consequently they regularly cycle through periods of indulgent bingeing, where they play excessively – followed by periods of self-loathing and purging – where they stop. The latter stage involving getting rid of games, deleting accounts or uninstalling software, etc., all before repurchasing, reinstalling and then overdoing it; going back round the cycle once again. The process can go on for long periods of time and results in the player feeling increasingly resentful toward both themselves and the games they are playing but powerless to effect a permanent change.

Another scenario I have encountered in clients is where the gamer has become aware of the negative impact of their gaming whilst they are actually gaming. This leads to a distinct sense of unease and discomfort with gaming that persists *even as they continue to play*. Sometimes they know what this reason is, sometimes they don't, but it feels almost life-threatening to consider switching off the power, despite the absence of enjoyment. The gaming feels at the same time both distasteful and inescapable. It has become their 'second job'; they don't like it, but it has to be done.

> *"I had stifled my passion for the game by burning myself out. The game no longer had any capacity for joy, only capacity for anger and self-loathing when I was defeated."*

Once a game starts to gain a pragmatic purpose such as this, it loses its status as a frivolous pastime. Effectively, it becomes *work*. It gains an importance on a deep, ontological level, on a par with foraging for scraps amidst a famine – players will play as if their life depended on it. As far as their unconscious is concerned, it does. In the above example it was pride that had led to this gamer feeling cornered into miserable play; were he to not game he would no longer be the best. Losing this status would call into question the months of work he had invested in the game, effectively posing the hollowing question, *'What was the point of that?'* Later, in the section on the causes of video game addiction, we will look in more depth at the existential fears that can motivate people to overuse games and find out more as to how gaming can transform into a matter of survival.

For now it is important for us to note that games, when played addictively, are frequently done so at the expense of their original purpose: to have fun and relax. Many gamers will experience the sense that they might enjoy themselves if they just defeat this next boss, find the next weapon or top the next league table. The games, cruelly, continue to promise enjoyment and satisfaction, but it is the experience of many addicted gamers that once they begin to scrutinize the time they spend gaming it is revealed as distinctly empty. The one, most powerful benefit of gaming (namely: pleasure) has somehow, subtly been stolen away.

CHAPTER TWO

The Signs of Video Game Addiction

While video game addiction is something that we are increasingly acknowledging, its recency makes it difficult to define. It is not uncommon for people to be living with a gamer or playing games themselves and thinking '*Is this ok?*'

Within the psychiatric community, most researchers and clinicians agree that games can be played to dysfunctional or pathological levels (Griffiths, 2011). Studies that have been carried out to find out how common the condition is tend to vary wildly, with figures suggesting between 3 percent to a little over 10 percent of gamers being candidates for addicted levels of video gaming (C. Ferguson 2011). A major problem with establishing reliable findings is that there is no formally recognized method for identifying when someone has a problem; hence the multitude of terms that are used to describe the condition (dysfunctional, heavy, excessive, problematic and, of course, addicted gaming). However, no matter how it is approached, the research tells us that for around 1 in 20 of us that decide to hit 'play', gaming can end up being carried in out a detrimental way.

On the surface, video game addiction appears to be about the amount of time spent gaming. This is certainly how it is broadly understood in the medical world. The

Council on Science and Public Health defined a 'heavy gamer' as any gamer that played for more than two hours a day (American Medical Association 2007). However, as with substance abuse, the quantity is not enough to determine if someone is or is not 'hooked'; someone who drinks 20 units a week across several social events but is otherwise able to get on with life is a totally different case from someone who becomes panicked and irate if they are unable to have their daily bottle of beer.

Definition: Abuse
Abusing a substance or behaviour involves deliberately overusing or taking a substance that you know to be harmful. It is crucially different from misuse in that the latter involves you using something that you did not know to be harmful (or perhaps thought was beneficial) in a damaging way. Video games cannot be abused, at least not in the way that substances can, whereby people often make use of them with the intent to harm themselves in someway.

Misuse
Misusing something, be it a drug or a behaviour, relies upon your initial belief that what you were doing was harmless or perhaps even good for you, and then using it in a damaging way. Video games are misused by people when they think that they will enhance their lives and end up being damaged by them. Abuse is something that is best reserved for substances and involves a wilful overuse with a potential intent to self-harm.

Addicted gaming will, invariably, involve a great deal of time spent gaming, but the actual indicators that something is wrong are both quite specific and not directly linked to time. Perhaps the most relevant and poignant sign is an increasing amount of palpable tension between the gamer and those close to them. Gaming addiction is crucially not a problem that solely involves the one playing games; it will be felt throughout the household – there will be a sense that something is wrong. Possibly it will be something that everyone is aware of and no-one is speaking about.

This tension will occasionally be expressed in anger and frustration when the gamer is separated from their gaming. This will be creating or aggravating an increasing distance between the gamer and others. At the same time as this increasing disconnect and potential friction, the gaming itself will appear, and be, more and more joyless. An almost painfully dedicated fixation or a crazed mania will accompany it – not the fun and pleasure that you might expect from someone engaging in their hobby.

A frequent situation is that of the rest of the household having given up on the gamer and simply accepting that they spend all their time gaming, that's what they do and there is nothing that can be done about it. Often this kind of resignation exists when a family or couple have gone through a protracted or particularly difficult period of tension after the loved ones attempted to extricate the gamer from the games and faced stiff resistance. It is important in these situations to recognise the ambivalence that often goes with addiction; just because they react badly to being pulled away from the games does not mean that they don't want you to try. It is in times like this that being close to an addict is a seemingly impossible test of your emotional stamina. As we will discuss later, the important step here is to find a middle ground between giving up and going on the offensive, both of which will only further the existing divide.

If an atmosphere such as that described above is present within your household, either focused on yourself or on someone you live with, then you may benefit from investigating the possibility of gaming addiction. We will now go a little deeper into exactly how gaming addiction is defined, breaking down the above description into a more distinct set of criteria, thereby clarifying the signs to watch for.

Discussion: Video Game Addiction as a Diagnosis
The concept of 'gaming addiction' has not formally been recognised as a psychiatric diagnosis. The American Psychological Association (APA), which compiles and writes the Diagnostic and Statistical Manual (DSM) – the American bible of mental illnesses – has not included 'gaming addiction' in the body of their latest edition, but instead added it to the "Speculative Section III" – effectively the appendix. By doing so, they are acknowledging it as being recommended for further study before it can be included into the main text (American Psychiatric Association 2013). By doing this, the APA appears to be acknowledging the youth of video gaming and is wisely being hesitant about rushing into applying a diagnosis. This is doubtless to allow the time required for the aforementioned moral panic surrounding the rapid advance of gaming addiction to settle into a more informed atmosphere – a stance that many social researchers agree with (Barnett and Coulson 2010).

Much of the difficulty that the APA faces is that there is no measure with which to usefully test for video game addiction. Most of the attempts thus far have been in some way based upon the diagnosis of gambling addiction that was included in the DSM IV (M. Griffiths 2008). Mark Griffiths of Nottingham Trent University, one of the chief authorities on the concept of gaming addiction, developed his own measure from the gambling template in the late '90s (Griffiths 1998). Kimberly Young, Founder and President of The Center for Internet Addiction (www.netaddiction.com), developed her internet addiction scale (IAT) in the same way (Young 1998). Young's scale has subsequently been adapted to try to encapsulate video gaming (Barnett et al. 2009). Beyond these are numerous tests of varying validity that have been put forward, none of which has effectively made the grade and ascended to the point of inclusion in either the DSM V or the ICD 10 – the international and unfortunately less used counterpart to the DSM (World Health Organisation 1992).

Griffiths, among others, has subsequently reviewed this uncomfortable reliance upon the gambling scale (Griffiths 2012). The main problem with the approach being, that what might be problematic for gambling, may not be problematic for gaming (C. Ferguson 2011). Take, for example, this gambling symptom: 'I use gambling to relax'. This means that should someone find themselves using gambling as a way to unwind or fill time then this person is potentially addicted to gambling. It is for good reasons that an attitude such as this is seen to be indicative of pathological gambling – this 'relaxing' is potentially losing me and my family uncontrollable amounts of money. Using a video game to relax, on the other hand, seems like as normal and functional way to engage with the medium as is conceivable. In fact, was someone to play a video game for a more pragmatic purpose they would be a riper candidate for the label of addict. The outcome of this medical tentativeness is that the status of 'gaming addiction' as a diagnosis is, at best, unofficial and shouldn't be considered a psychiatric certainty – whatever such a thing may be.

The Six Signs of Video Game Addiction

Simply playing a lot of video games does not, in itself, indicate addiction; the difference is qualitative not quantitative. *How* you play games is more important to determining gaming addiction than *how much* you play games. Mark Griffiths, mentioned above, understands addiction through six lenses, or criteria, all of which come together to form a definition. In any individual where these are all present, addiction has taken hold (Griffiths 2008). Van Cleave (2010), a self-revealed "World of Warcraft" addiction survivor, took Griffith's six criteria and very usefully applied them directly to the subject of video gaming.

The six criteria, as Van Cleave described them, are: **salience, mood modification, tolerance, withdrawal symptoms, conflict** and **relapse**. These give a solid starting point from which we can begin to understand what it looks like for someone to be playing games to an unhealthy level. These criteria capture the mental takeover that happens when gaming becomes all-important for someone, the subtle and overt battles with others as they constantly try to make time for gaming and finally the difficulty some people have in maintaining a restriction on their gaming.

The signs that are put forward in this book are a development of the criteria as presented by Griffiths and Van Cleave. For the sake of clarity I have used the same headings for each of the six, though the details are in some cases altered. While the original six criteria are an excellent building block, they can be importantly developed in a few areas. This is largely owing to some remaining translation scars where the symptoms used were adapted from the symptoms for gambling (see the previous discussion). Additionally, the descriptions have been expanded and evolved to cover the newer forms and methods of mobile and appointment-based gaming.

Now we will go through each of the signs. For each one I have provided a description of how this is most likely to manifest in someone's world. This will most likely allow you to measure the behaviour of someone close to you to see if gaming addiction is present. Equally, gamers themselves might benefit from checking their own behaviours, thoughts and feelings against the six signs.

Salience

The gaming has become the most important part of the gamer's life. The majority of their thoughts and desires are now about the game.

Salience is perhaps the most readily identifiable of all of the signs for the gamer themselves. For those of us that are heavily into gaming or any other highly involved hobby, spending much of your day dreaming about gaming is an assumption, even a pleasure of the lifestyle. Lessons/meetings that grow dull are kept alive by a constant musing on what you will be doing next in the game.

Having something that we love to spend time thinking about feels, much like infatuation, like a positive and healthy way to live life. For this reason it is important to emphasise salience in terms of its most negative aspects, chiefly how it might lead to distancing us from others and manifest as an uncomfortable craving that makes life outside of gaming hard to notice or have time for.

To re-iterate a point made earlier, salience is not just about a player spending most of their time gaming. It is about them being unable to do anything but focus on the game for at least the majority of the day. This might manifest as them being distracted as they plan their next move, holding on to their phone as they wait for the next gaming appointment or immersing themselves in gaming paraphernalia when they can't get to the game itself; all to the exclusion of life outside.

What does this mean for the gamer? Salience is all consuming. Life becomes about video gaming – it is the goal toward which all things point. The world becomes divided into two phenomena, gaming and things that get in the way of gaming. Anything that falls into the latter category is conducted with haste and impatience; food is bolted, work is rushed, walking becomes closer to running and conversations are injected with the impatience required to ensure that they can be broken off at the earliest opportunity.

How does this appear to others? If you are living with someone for whom gaming has become salient then you will get the distinct feeling that you have somehow become an inconvenience. In the main this is because they are spending as much time as possible gaming – and this can be intimidating lengths of time, up to 70 or 80 hours a week and comfortably spanning entire days and nights. Innocuous and unthreatening exchanges from others are met with impatience and brevity. While the gamer is away from their device they will be pre-occupied with thoughts of gaming – distracted and showing signs that they are planning their next return to playing.

Mood Modification

The gamer's emotional state becomes heavily influenced by gaming to the point whereby they appear to need the game in order to control their moods.

Discussion: The Fear of Fun

Descriptions of 'mood modification' often specify either a 'buzz' or a 'numbing' as symptoms of addicted gaming. Whilst becoming numb is an undesirable state to accompany any activity, feeling a 'buzz' is a very healthy response. Indeed, feeling a rush of excitement or happiness is largely the goal of games. In gaming psychology the term often used to describe the buzz felt from gaming is fiero, a Spanish word for a sense of achievement and overcoming that has no fitting English equivalent.

Fiero, alongside a range of emotions that gaming is likely to produce, should not be quickly pathologised. For gamers this is one of the truest expressions of games at their best – a feeling that is intended by both developers and gamers. This will most often be seen as sudden explosions of boisterous yet harmless delight, much the same as when a footballer scores an important goal.

There are a host of research studies dedicated to detailing the health and educational advantages of playing video games (Warburton et al. 2007, Squire et al 2003). According to studies such as these, reactions are improved, creative thinking is learned, senescence is kept at bay, education is made accessible, violent emotions are expunged. Very rarely, if at all, do you see an academic crediting video games with being enjoyable and fun to play; it is as if acknowledging that the sense of fun or fiero generated by gaming is taboo. It would seem that finding fun in something that is not somehow progressive or altruistic is somehow seen as pathological.

Peter Toohey, in his book *Boredom: A Lively History*, talks of the 'tyranny of pragmatism'; he argues that in Western culture an activity needs to have a constructive purpose if it is to be considered justifiable. If an activity is done simply for fun, then it is commonly seen as wasted time (Toohey 2011).

It is important to not misinterpret mood modification. A gamer's mood should be modified to some degree when they play a game; they should enjoy themselves, become immersed, marvel at the spectacles, curse their controller in defeat and punch the air in victory. The important aspect of mood modification as a criterion for addiction is not so much what moods are created, but that the gamer is dependent upon gaming in order to regulate and manage their moods.

For the gaming addict, playing has stopped being a want and turned into a need. As we will go on to describe more later on, there is typically an external pressure that is driving the gamer out of the external world and into the gaming world. The game has become, to the gamer, a mother to a distressed newborn; without it, they are troubled, anxious, depressed or angry, and with it, they can become jubilant, relieved or simply 'feed' in a state of numbness.

A common flashpoint at which this manifests is when the gamer is separated from gaming, either through enforced commitments, loss of connection, broken hardware or zero charge on a phone. If these instances lead to a notable decline in mood and the subsequent reuniting suddenly has a powerful uplifting or anaesthetising effect then the gamer is displaying the signs for mood modification.

What does this mean for the gamer? Moods become heavily influenced by whether or not you are gaming. When you are not gaming you are desperate and rushed to get back to it, with a sense that the world has suddenly become difficult to cope with. Each time gaming is resumed it is a relief, a soothing or even joyous return to 'normality'. During gaming, feelings both emotional and physical tend to be put to one side – they can comfortably be ignored for hours at a time.

How does this appear to others? People living with addicted gamers often speak of a transformation in their son/husband/wife, etc. It is as if they no longer recognize them when they are playing. They appear to be over-involved in the game. This can manifest as a manic attention to the game or conversely they may play with a complete lack of emotion. Both will involve them finding it incredibly difficult to drag their attention away from the game. Being with the gamer when they are playing, as opposed to when they are not playing, is like being with two different people.

Tolerance

The gamer is never satisfied by the games; either perpetually playing the same game or constantly cycling through many different games.

In healthy gaming, as we play, our tolerance to its wonders increases until we ultimately cannot get any more, at which point we move on. A well-designed game will drip feed its features to you throughout the experience, constantly giving you something new to play with and master. In most cases, this will eventually run dry. For the engaged gamer, this often comes about upon completing a game; something that can result in a perfectly acceptable period of mourning the end of the game, much as we might feel sad upon completion of a good novel.

When a player has reached a point of perpetually 'searching' for engagement in gaming, then they have become tolerant to gaming. Whatever they do now, it is no longer enough. There are two ways in which this is typically expressed. The most predominant form of this is for a player to endlessly play the same game, long after they have seen everything that the game meaningfully has to offer. This might mean a never-ending collection of every minor achievement in "World of Warcraft", many of which require a colossal investment of time spent repeating the same actions. Alternatively it could be the continual expansion of one's empire in "Clash of Clans", repeatedly contesting with like-minded players for the same coveted positions at the top of the league tables.

Definition: Achievements
First devised by Microsoft, achievements are a form of meta-game. They create a game around another game by rewarding you for certain actions. For example, you get an

achievement for finding all the secrets in Tomb Raider, although this reward does not, in itself, provide any bonus in the game. They have been criticized for allowing developers to extend the amount of time gamers play by asking them to secure very difficult or very time-consuming achievements.

The second and less obvious form of addiction is for the gamer to constantly be playing new games, cycling through them at a rapid rate, in which they are never fully engaging with any one of them. Gamers following this pattern are often in a state of being jaded with the games industry itself, constantly seeking the same joy they received from games they enjoyed when they were younger. What the gamer doesn't see in this position is that it is not the quality of the games that has disappeared, but the quality of their engagement. Whereas they used to dedicate time and attention to games until they became deeply meaningful, they now skim across the surface, fixating on what they can play next and lamenting that the current game is not instantly giving them the same feeling of wonder they once felt.

What does this mean for the gamer? If you compare the quality of gaming now to how it was when you first discovered it, it will feel strangely empty. The frequency with which you actually experience joy or fun in the game is now a rare or entirely lost feeling, though you are typically spurred on by the *prospect* of that fun, more than any sense of actually *having* fun. Gaming feels like it's constantly about to get good, though on reflection, the amount of times that it actually *is* good is strangely low. Gaming has become tough, dedicated work.

How does this appear to others? You no longer get a sense of the gamer *enjoying* themselves when they game. The hallmarks of fun have drained away to be replaced by a kind of fixated 'searching' for fun. They might have a single game that they play endlessly, possibly for years on end. Alternatively, they might have hundreds of games that they rapidly move through, either physically stacking up in the house or in the form of hundreds of downloaded games on their portable device or online game platform.

Discussion: Misunderstandings around Tolerance in Gaming Addiction

Much of the existing academic literature states that criteria of tolerance is displayed when the gamer needs to play for longer and longer periods of time in order to reach the same high or buzz from a game (Griffiths 2008). The implication being that there is a certain desired state that takes gamers longer and longer to reach as they play more and more, as if their 'buzz' tank begins all play sessions at 'empty' and then gradually fills as they play. In my work with gaming addicts, and certainly from my own past experiences, this does not accurately capture what it means to become tolerant to gaming.

By ascribing tolerance to the need to play for longer and longer, the foundational models of gambling and substance abuse have led to a slight misapplication of symptoms, one that does not fit with the actuality of video game addiction. This is an important mistake to avoid, as it implies that the duration someone plays for should be used as a symptom in diagnosing video game addiction. As we have said before, it is *how* they play that matters, not *how much* they play.

Philip Zimbardo and Nikita Duncan, in their book and

TED talk, 'The Demise of Guys', offer a different understanding of tolerance in gaming, as opposed to a more conventional substance-based understanding:

> *We can think of them as "arousal addictions." A major source of the continual arousal, whether it is in the cortex or the testes, is the novelty, the variety or the surprise factor of the content. Sameness is soon habituated; differentness is attention sustaining. And the video game and porn industries are supplying a virtually endless variety of variety.*
> **—Zimbardo & Duncan, 2012**

To an extent this is correct. The games played to the most excessive levels are generally roleplaying games or RPGs (Nagygyorgy et al 2013), all of which work around the looting mechanic, in which you kill a monster, get a random bunch of goodies, kill another monster, get another random bunch of goodies. Again, this mechanic, known as *variable reward scheduling*, crucially relies upon getting different rewards all the time, and constantly chasing the next, potentially lucrative, kill. In addition, the most addictive of games will allow players to play the same game quite literally 'endlessly', by always ensuring there is something new to do. Zimbardo suggests that gamers generate a tolerance to 'sameness' that can only be broken through repeatedly finding new rewards in the game.

Somewhat in contradiction, however, is the reality that the most typical addicted gamers will tend to stick to the same game for long, long periods of time, typically repeating similar actions over and over again. It is when a game becomes largely predictable and yet still keeps the attention that addiction becomes a risk. This is a sign that the game has become safe, and is now acting as a refuge.

Gambling, porn and substance abuse are concepts from which we can usefully start to construct models of addicted gaming, but they inevitably bring some misdirection by failing to capture the unique nature of misusing video games. What addicted gamers become tolerant to is the challenge. If a player has reached gold, they will want platinum. If they have reached the highest level in a game, they will want the best equipment for their character. If they have earned nine achievements they will want 10, and so on. Likewise, if they have completed this game, then they will now want to complete that game, then that game, and so on. For the healthy, dedicated gamer, each new goal typically involves further and further investments of time and higher and higher levels of challenge as the targets become more difficult to reach. This continues until they are satisfied with what they have accomplished or become disinterested. The addicted gamer grows tolerant to the sense of reward, but continues to remain fixated.

Withdrawal Symptoms

When the gamer finds themselves unable to play they suffer from negative emotional states such as irritability, sadness or anxiety.

Dependency of all kinds is always characterized by the apparent overreaction to losing the object of the dependency. In the case of video games, this means that when the game is either switched off or otherwise becomes inaccessible, the gamer becomes disproportionately distressed or angry. This plays out equally in situations whereby the game can't be played, such as when you are out visiting friends or on holiday. Withdrawal is one of the signs that adapts very smoothly from other models of addiction to video game addiction.

Addiction, being primarily about expectancy, leads sufferers to establish patterns in their lives that allow them to constantly focus on when they will next get access to their behaviour of choice. Withdrawal symptoms will often occur when the gamer should be able to game, according to the patterns of play they are used to, but is for whatever reason denied. For example, take a situation where the gamer was used to rushing home from work and then switching on the PC, then one evening they arrived back to find that they had visitors whom they were required to help entertain. If addiction is present in this gamer then the expectation around gaming that has built up over the last eight hours or so will express itself, most likely as a sullenness but possibly as an out-of-character causticity. If the addiction is powerful enough, they will go ahead and game, regardless of the social consequences.

The emotional states that can manifest are varied. Perhaps most notably are outbursts of anger, which are particularly likely when the gamer is suddenly and forcibly stopped from gaming. Other than this, a moroseness, apathy and agitation are all likely. These can, as with all powerful emotions, express themselves physically in the form of the shakes or sweating. All these emotions, while expressing a distress at the withdrawal of gaming, also serve a tactical purpose, whether the gamer is aware of it or not. They all work to punish those around them for not enabling the gaming. Frequently they can be so effective at doing this that family and friends can settle for letting the addiction have its way rather than risk facing the withdrawal symptoms.

Withdrawal symptoms and mood modification are frequently two sides of the same coin and come hand in hand. The first is about how they react when they are not gaming (or more specifically, when gaming is abruptly discontinued) and the latter is about how they react when they are gaming. Put together the two signs show a person that is agitated when away from games, and preoccupied and over-involved when they are gaming.

What does this mean for the gamer? Any upcoming period of time in which you won't be able to game becomes an object of worry, causing you to go to great lengths to re-establish contact with the gaming world, even if this means demonstrating extreme emotions to those around you in order to get your way. You'll allow yourself to become quite out of control when deprived of gaming, as it frequently will get you what you want. Should your gaming ever be cut short, you are likely to react explosively and possibly aggressively.

How does this appear to others? Perhaps the most demonstrative way in which this will become clear is if you have ever, having reached the end of your wits, decided to forcefully interrupt the gaming and been faced with a shockingly distressed, aggressive or possibly even violent reaction. More commonly, you will notice that when the gamer is, for whatever reason, prevented from playing, they become noticeably more anxious, gloomy or angry, or a mix of these three.

Conflict
The gamer finds themselves frequently arguing with or trying to deceive others when it comes to the subject of their gaming habits.
Conflict, in many ways, is the most powerful manifestation of video game addiction. Life becomes a

battle between gaming and the forces that threaten to prevent gaming, putting the gamer at odds with the non-gaming world. In fighting this battle, the gamer will, like any addict, begin to use a remarkably diverse and sophisticated array of manipulations to get what they want: lying, faking, arguing, rudeness, hiding, flattery, malingering, shouting, sulking – whatever works. It isn't long before people either catch on to the ploys or grow sick of the ways in which they are being treated, at which point conflict is sparked, if it isn't already present.

Addicts of all kinds will typically demonstrate an incredible ability to manipulate situations in order to maximise the amount of time they are able to indulge themselves. Other people become objects to be manoeuvred in order to make as much room as possible. One of the most basic ways to do this is to bully or overreact to them whenever gaming is questioned. Addicted gamers who feel like they are less powerful than the other person are more likely to revert to more subtle means.

What does this mean for the gamer? Other people, aside from those you game with, have become obstacles and nothing more. Each one now represents a possible risk to your gaming time: your mother might require you come to the table for a meal, your wife might suggest a day out, your children might ask that you play with them. Somewhere along the line your priorities have shifted toward shutting down these threats in the most efficient way possible. Perhaps if you become rude enough at the table they won't want you there anymore, perhaps if you act distant and dismissive when you go out with your wife she won't risk another day together and hopefully by shouting at your children they won't dare interrupt you again. No matter whom you fight with and how, whether you get your way or not, you come away feeling horrible and the best solution is always to game. The times you will actively engage with those close to you are often due to your exploiting an opportunity to create gaming time: *'I think you owe it to yourself to go out, darling, you've worked so hard recently. I'll be fine here.'*

How does this appear to others? Where you used to have a positive relationship with the gamer, this is now rarely possible. You find yourself forced to make a tough decision on a daily basis: do you enjoy the relative calm and sense of 'keeping the peace' by allowing them to ignore you in favour of their gaming or do you risk seeking a little intimacy and face an inevitable onslaught of sullenness or even aggression? You may also have the sinking realisation that the times when you seem to be getting along are actually instances when you are being 'set up' and allowing the gamer to game without you getting in the way.

Relapse
The gamer has previously made attempts to control their gaming, either with or without the support of others, but has always reverted back to excessive gaming.

A fundamental aspect of addiction is that the will to deviate or stop the damaging behaviour is either too weak or simply too absent to have any effect in itself. This means that, at some point, the gamer acknowledges the need to cut back or stop their gaming, only to never actually make the change or find themselves drawn back into problematic or addicted levels of gaming.

For some gamers, this can lead to the 'binge-purge cycle' whereby they switch between gaming excessively, hating themselves, and then stopping for a period before beginning again. While they can see, quite clearly, that gaming is hurting their lives, they don't seem to be able to divert from this pattern, at least not for any length of time.

What does this mean for the gamer? It has, to some degree, become apparent that gaming is an issue for you, either through your own self-reflection or by having to relent to the constant pressure of someone close to you. Furthermore, it is clear that you don't appear to be able to stop. This has led you to dislike yourself for your lack of willpower and sometimes even harbour a grudge against the games you play while playing them.

How does this appear to others? Even though you have managed, at times, to persuade the gamer to see just how negative their gaming has become, any commitment to change never seems to last. Perhaps they limit the gaming for several days or even weeks but, in the end, they always go straight back to excessive gaming. It is as if they are on a collision course and simply cannot or do not want to make a long term decision to change course.

Using the Six Signs
The six signs provide a benchmark against which to judge the severity of either your own gaming or the gaming of someone close to you. If all of the signs are present to intrusive levels and are causing upset or preventing day-to-day functioning, then there is the strong possibility of video game addiction. It is important to remember that

this is not a formal method of diagnosis. Not even a psychiatrist would be able to do that due to the absence of there being any current diagnostic recognition of video gaming addiction as a disorder.

An important distinction to make is between *problematic gaming* and *gaming addiction*. This is key language in video game addiction theory that enables us to establish a guideline between different levels of severity. Much confusion comes about on account of not acknowledging or adhering to this terminology (Griffiths 2014).

Problematic gaming is when someone's gaming habits partially interfere with their life, but not to a pervasive level. As a guideline, if someone is exhibiting one but not all of the signs of addiction then they are likely to be gaming to problematic levels. Because of the vague nature of problematic gaming, it is likely that many gamers are in fact problematic gamers. If someone is gaming problematically then their life will likely improve if they develop a healthier attitude toward their gaming, though the issue is unlikely to be urgent or be putting other areas of their life at risk.

Gaming addiction is when someone's gaming habits have taken over their life to the point where they have jeopardized or destroyed important social ties such as their love life, their role as a parent or their work. It is likely to have lead to an emotional deadening and in some cases poor physical health on account of the time spent gaming. Gaming addicts will display all the signs of addiction. In some cases, all the signs bar relapse might be present, in which case it is best to assume that the gamer is addicted; you will often not know how severe the situation is until a first attempt at controlling play has been attempted and then failed. Gaming addiction is a serious issue that you should seek support in managing.

The Six Signs of Video Game Addiction

Salience	The gaming has become the most important part of the gamer's life. The majority of their thoughts and desires are now about the game.
Mood Modification	The gamer's emotional state becomes heavily influenced by gaming to the point whereby they appear to need the game in order to control their moods.
Tolerance	The gamer is never satisfied by the games, either perpetually playing the same game or constantly cycling through many different games.
Conflict	The gamer finds themselves frequently arguing with or trying to deceive others when it comes to the subject of their gaming habits.
Withdrawal	When the gamer finds themselves unable to play they suffer from negative emotional states such as irritability, sadness or anxiety.
Relapse	The gamer has previously made attempts to control their gaming, either with or without the support of others, but has always reverted back to excessive gaming.

CHAPTER THREE

What Causes Video Game Addiction?

Billions of people play games every year. As noted earlier, in the gloomiest of calculations, up to 10 percent of these qualify as playing to the point where it has become dangerous, excessive or addictive. Why is it that some people end up playing to damaging levels and most do not?

This section covers the controversial and sticky subject of what triggers and maintains addiction, more specifically video game addiction. It considers a number of possibilities, notably that addiction is an illness that some of us suffer, that some of us have a personality that inclines us toward overuse, that games deliberately breed addiction or that our situation leads some of us to choose addiction as a working solution. Finally, we look at how one might bring together all of these ideas into a single more holistic understanding.

This section is primarily discursive and should be treated so. The views presented here are offered as food for thought and any consideration of a cause should be done out of curiosity as there is a considerable emotional charge in this topic. Any investigation into a cause often comes from wanting to know who to blame. If the cause is environmental, then we might feel we can blame parents and loved ones; if it's disease, we can blame the universe; if it's games, then we can blame the developers; if it's personality, then we have a choice of either ourselves or the universe, depending on how we want to look at it.

When wanting to dig into the cause of gaming addiction, either in relation to yourself as a gamer, a loved one, or as a parent or a counsellor, consider *which cause you are hoping to find*. More than likely you have already decided and are hoping that the next section will validate your views. Perhaps you want to find that your unloving parents are guilty for your gaming addiction so you can remove the responsibility from yourself, or perhaps you want to find games as the culprit for your client's addiction to reinforce your own discomfort in a world of technology you feel increasingly alienated by. Check your investments – exposing them to yourself will be nothing other than useful to you.

I offer four causes in this section. The first is the disease model of addiction. The second looks at the addictive personality and the third considers the extent to which games lead to addiction. The final cause I put forward is that of the gamer's own choice to escape from either an internal or an external world that they find unbearable; this is the position that I tentatively work from most frequently, although I feel it prudent to maintain an openness to the other perspectives.

To look at the cause of addiction is unavoidably tangled up with looking at the definition of addiction. This section is, if you like, as much about deciding what is meant by addiction as it is about determining how it comes about.

Cause One: Addiction as a Disease

Perhaps the most widely recognised model of addiction considers it to be a disease of the mind. This was the fundamental idea in Wilson's "Big Book", the cornerstone of Alcoholics Anonymous (AA) (Wilson 1939). This has been academically developed over the years, with studies showing concrete changes in the brain of the addict, lending weight to the position (Berke 2000). It is from the disease model that the AA developed their first and primarily curative step for all addicts: admitting that you are powerless to control your drinking. The disease is in fact in control of your actions, not you.

The disease model of drinking has been inflated to cover all addiction (Rosecrance 1985-1986); leading to the widespread understanding that once you have passed a certain threshold of using any given habit (once you have the *disease* of addiction) any control over the habit is lost. Not only that, but control is lost permanently. This would mean that if someone struggled with addictive gaming in the past then, once recovered, they would be unable to return to healthy levels of gaming. This is certainly the lived experience of some gaming addicts such as Andrew Doan, author of *Hooked on Games*. Doan very much found that even after a long period of abstaining from games, when he went back to play the habit once again consumed his life. For Doan, playing in a controlled or moderated way was simply not an option.

Definition: Abstinence

To abstain is to give up an addictive behaviour entirely. Many people and addiction theorists believe this to be the only effective method of dealing with addiction, including video game addiction. For some people who become addicted to games, any return to gaming will lead to a relapse. For these people, abstinence is the only option.

The most prominent objection to the disease model of addiction is that it denies responsibility from the addict (Fingarette 1988). An addict, under the disease model, is considered helpless in the face of their illness and typically needs to give themselves up to a higher power – normally this means God (the AA model is a religious model) and/or medical professionals. They are effectively removed from the equation. The gamer has to resign to not being able to make a difference. If we are to consider themselves games in this way, then the gaming addict, once he has crossed that line, is no longer accountable for the decision to keep gaming.

This disease model runs the risk of allowing the gamer to disown his habit thereby, in some cases, perpetuating the problem. The gamer can shirk all responsibility for the gaming, lament his condition, wait for others to do the work and in the meantime, game.

Another drawback to the disease model's application is that in advocating the permanence of the condition, health services are effectively making recovery synonymous with never playing another video game. In essence, this tells addicted gamers, 'If you are successfully treated then you will never play a game again'. While gamers who have a full blown addiction are most likely to benefit from this approach, the message can deter many problematic gamers from ever making contact with professionals lest they find themselves permanently severed from their favourite hobby.

There is increasing evidence that this approach does

not sit well with the issue of gaming. Keith Bakker, from the Smith & Jones Clinic in Amsterdam, where they have been treating addiction to video gaming since 2006, changed tack after a couple of years of working with the young people using the disease model of addiction. He subsequently claimed that the evidence they had gathered implied that the condition was better treated from a paradigm of choice, rather than that of a disease (MacGuire 2008).

While there are a number of philosophical and pragmatic drawbacks to the disease model of addiction, it can be the only path to recovery for a few particularly acute cases. There are a minority of addicted gamers who will simply never be able to pick up a game without getting sucked back into addicted play. For these people, it is best that they come to terms with themselves as having a disease, one that they can control, post recovery, by understanding that abstinence is the only cure and that they can never go back to games. For most addicted gamers, however, promoting their responsibility to manage their gaming is an important, valuable and accessible attitude toward getting better.

Discussion: Addiction and the Concept of Freedom

Twelve-step programmes, chiefly AA, have been hugely successful in dealing with substance abuse. As a result, much of their philosophy has become hard-baked into the definition of addiction. The idea that addicts are powerless and that they are not responsible is one that the 12-step programmes have always propagated and one that many people have accepted as fact (Wilson 1939). Indeed, such doctrines consider this initial admission fundamental to the healing process (Washton 1989). Perhaps the biggest issue with this idea is that it raises very awkward questions about our freedom as human beings. In suggesting that the addict has no power, it infers that any effort they make is futile, something that no one believes. Ultimately, the addict is the one that has to work the hardest in order to break out of their behaviour. The disease model denies the addict their freedom, saying that the drink/game is making the decisions for them.

I work therapeutically with a belief in the freedom of the human spirit, in its ultimate capacity to choose for itself how it responds to the situations it finds itself in. If someone games into the early hours of the morning at the expense of their children, spouse and work, then that is an action that *they* are choosing. While I can empathize with and recognise the immense external pressures that this person may be under, I cannot attribute the final decision to anything other than the individual. This comes from an assumption that we are fundamentally free to make our own decisions. The concept of free will is a hugely contentious argument and one that I would derail this book by entering into. Suffice it to say, it is my leap of faith as a human being and as a psychotherapist; I believe us all to be ultimately (and somewhat absurdly) free.

From this point of view, gaming addiction can be understood as someone regularly considering gaming to be the best possible course of action, even when it appears to others to be nothing but harmful. Even if their partner is threatening to leave them, or they are going to flunk their exam tomorrow, gaming might still come out as being the preferable course of action. While this might not seem to make any sense, it is perhaps because we do not share that person's sense of hopelessness that even if they did do the 'right thing', they would still be abandoned, or still fail their exam. At the very least, gaming might distract them from these apparent inevitabilities. In these instances, the gamer hasn't been forced to game against their better judgement. Nearly the reverse: their judgement (albeit not their better one) has led them to game.

Cause Two: The Addictive Personality

The addictive personality model considers there to be certain personalities that are more prone to becoming addicted than others. These people have common traits that correlate with excess of some kind. Many research studies have looked into identifying these correlations in character, particularly in relation to substance abuse (Jacobs 1971, Nathan 1988). These studies have identified common traits such as anti-social behaviour, social withdrawal and negative perceptions of their mother as occurring frequently in substance addicts.

A recent study in Japan concluded that the two behaviours commonly found in addicted online gamers were that of rumination and short-term thinking (Wang 2013). The addictive personality model would, following this, suggest that young people who were inclined to spend time going over and over thoughts in their head, as well as struggling to organise mid to long-term plans, would be more inclined to end up playing games to addictive levels.

The addictive personality model suffers somewhat from 'chicken and egg syndrome', in that it has a tough job proving that the aspects it finds in addicts were there prior to the addiction, and not that it was in fact the addiction that brought on these common characteristics. The latter seems highly likely, certainly in an instance such as video gaming, whereby all involved have typically been in the same socially-distanced and game-fuelled environment for much of their lives and are thereby highly likely to have picked up mirroring behaviours and attitudes.

Across the clients I have worked with I have not seen a great deal of evidence for the existence of unifying traits that bring these people together. I would certainly say they are more likely to be men, and, further, more likely to be young men. Aspects of personality that are the same are not frequently obvious, however. Certainly the characteristics associated with substance abuse don't present themselves. I have never encountered anti-social behaviour as being a common correlate with problematic video gaming; this is more exclusively related to substance abuse. Neither have I noticed any regularly negative perceptions of the mother, at least nothing over and above what is standard. If anything, where negative perceptions of the parent exist, they are aimed at the father. At the same time this is not uncommon in clients — few of us report a wholly comfortable relationship with our parents.

One factor that is commonplace is social withdrawal. Addictive video gamers all report a significant discomfort in social situations and groups, something that they have been aware of long before the gaming became salient. Often, these individuals will be happy to take part in groups online, but large face-to-face encounters are daunting and generally avoided. Also, in agreement with the findings of Wang's research, I have found every addicted gamer to be very thoughtful and reflective, far more comfortable mulling over a problem rather than taking action. This is largely the mindset to which gaming appeals; people that are more action-orientated often find games require far more patience and understanding than they care to commit.

In many ways the addictive personality model shares similarities with the disease model in that it distances the responsibility from the gamer, allowing them to blame their inherent or genetic build rather than to ascribe the behaviour to a choice that they are making. However, unlike the disease model, the addictive personality model implies that the sufferer can make decisions regarding how they manage their personality. They might be inclined to have the urge to game when they shouldn't, but that doesn't mean they can't override this. This perspective tells us that while certain people can be prone to addiction, they can potentially find a moderated return to their habit at some point in the future.

Cause Three: Video Games

As with any addiction or excess, it is important to investigate the degree to which the behaviour itself is responsible: be it alcohol, sex, cocaine or video games. There is a temptation to lay the blame entirely at the feet of the behaviour. Many would argue that this point of view is unhelpful in the way it diverts responsibility away from the user toward an activity that is frequently impossible, impractical or dangerous to try and prohibit (Kuchera 2013). South Korea has, through several recent laws, gone about trying to prohibit gaming to addicted levels. Some players break the law to get around it, some abide by it and many of them are outraged by this imposition. Nonetheless, the viewpoint that 'Games cause addiction' prevails in both the media and much of mainstream thinking and has merit enough to be worth considering.

Many of the more damning portrayals of gaming, such as the aforementioned 2010 "Panorama" episode, will construct much of their case by putting a negative spin on the fact that games are designed to be enjoyable. This perspective suggests that game development studios are doing something nefarious when they do their best to create content that is as compelling and exciting as possible. Panorama revealed that games rely upon certain mechanics, such as the 'variable reward', to keep players engaged. It is not uncommon for critics of video games to isolate a psychological mechanism used by game developers and hold it up as being created with the intention of unfairly keeping players' interest. This is much the same as accusing movie makers of optimizing the camerawork of their films in order to make their movies as compelling as possible.

Nonetheless, there is a difference, in gaming, between making a good game and making an addictive game. This is largely the concern of developers, and something that I will address later. Games and gaming studios are not guilty of creating addiction just because they are working from any understanding of human thinking. It should be no surprise to us that these people know a lot more about how we think than we do; it is only from this knowledge that they can produce the finest possible products. However, when they employ mechanics that detract from the enjoyment of the game in order to retain the gamer, then they are creating something that is arguable unhealthy and unethical. It is not that they are using tricks; it is the nature of the tricks that matters.

The terminology of 'variable rewards' refers to Burrhus Frederic Skinner and his famed 'Skinner boxes', typically containing rats. This is a very well known piece of pop psychology: Skinner's rats are wheeled out in books and articles on their own rather regular schedule. The notion of variable rewards is perhaps the most frequently cited mechanic when discussing how games go about addicting the gamer – as a result it bears discussing further.

Skinner wanted to find out the conditions under which a creature would repeat an action. For this experiment he made use of rats, rewarding them, in varying ways, when they performed certain actions; typically pressing a lever with their nose. The showcase discovery of Skinner's experiments being that rats were most likely to press the lever when they were rewarded for their actions *at random*. If a rat was rewarded with food every time it hit the lever it would soon stop once it had its fill. However, if the food only appeared every now and again following the press of a lever, the rat would hammer away at it, generating far more food than it needed. The conclusion being that an action that is rewarded on a variable schedule is inherently compelling (Skinner 1957), regardless of the nature of the reward itself.

This finding has been adapted into a game feature that can be found in nearly every game in existence today (and has always been the erratically beating heart of gambling). Match Three games such as "Candy Crush Saga" and "Bejewelled" respond to our moves with dazzling fireworks and explosions, but only *some of the time*. All roleplaying games, with negligible exceptions, have random drops of loot coming out of the bad guys when they die; sometimes you will find nothing, sometimes you will find a unique and ultra-rare weapon – you never know. All such games are making constant and liberal use of the variable reward mechanic.

Those who consider games to be the main culprit in
gaming addiction suggest that the use of psychological
breakthroughs, such as Skinner's research, has led to the
recent brainwashing of all contemporary gamers. Doan,
a physician and self-confessed gaming addict, described
the use of variable rewards in games as providing the
"digital heroin for my mind" (Doan 2012). What this and
Panorama don't acknowledge is that this feature has
existed in games for centuries. Skinner only put into
scientific literature what had already been cemented in
game design since before recorded history. Consider dice:
used in Ancient Egypt to play games, and still a
fundamental tool in gaming today. The cast of a die
involves an action (rolling) and leads to a variable reward
(*Will I get a 1 or a 6?*). Cards, more recently, rely upon
this. Typically, with each new draw from the deck, you
have a chance to get a card that doesn't help you, or one
that does, possibly even winning the game for you.
Skinner didn't discover a game mechanic; he merely
described one of the ways in which games have always
worked.

Games are designed to be fun and engaging; it should
be no surprise to find out that they have particular
methods of achieving this. McGonigal describes them as
'Happiness Engines', wherein the developers are tasked
with creating as much flow and engagement as possible
(McGonigal 2011). There is a temptation to pathologise
the feeling of fun that people are, by design, eliciting from
gaming, even though someone feeling a buzz or sense of
enjoyment is an entirely natural response to gaming.

While games should not be wholly demonized as
causing gaming addiction, it is, at the same time,
important to acknowledge that games are a potential

object for addiction, albeit one that is comparatively free of risk, unlike cocaine or gambling. Games have, long before their computerized versions, always had the power to distract and immerse. The combination of games and technology understandably offers a powerful medium for losing oneself.

Not all games are equally likely to spark addiction in a gamer, as we outlined previously. The games that are most notorious for this are online roleplaying games, such as "World of Warcraft" and "Eve". The next most likely are online shooters such as "Halo" and "Call of Duty". Finally, the other category that is often linked to addiction is the real time strategy: examples include "Starcraft" and the "Command and Conquer" series. Notably, these are all games played online and thereby (Nagygyorgy 2013) with others, something we'll consider later on.

There are, in my experience as a game designer, plenty of freemium development studios out there that don't give due consideration to addiction and, generally unwittingly but sometimes very deliberately, many studios that actually aim to twist the lives of their users until every waking hour and every dollar they earn is poured into the game. In the business, these players are called whales. Whales are the high spending one percent of an audience that are funding the game for everyone else to enjoy either free or at minimal cost. A company with a healthy attitude considers whales to be dedicated and wealthy fans of the game that get the most out of their experience by paying. A company with a less healthy attitude considers them the rich addicts. Studios that make games designed to hurt and extort their players generally make terrible games that go nowhere. On the whole, a game designed to addict is a bad game and players will know when they are being manipulated and quit.

There are a number of design decisions that I think go into many successful games these days that unfairly angle games toward addicting their players. In the final section of this book I offer a brief guide to developers as to how to design games to be non-addictive. What I will do here is to lay out, in layman's terms, the types of games that I think you should be cautious of.

Games that rely upon rewarding you to entertain you. Games today often give out rewards to the players on a regular basis. These could be resources (gold, gems or mana), objects (swords, buildings, vehicles) or abilities (spells, attack moves or powers). With any game, consider if you would enjoy playing that game if you had all the rewards from the start; would it still be fun to play? If the answer is yes, then the game is one that you are genuinely engaging with. If the answer is no, then you are playing solely for the expectation of a reward. This is a notoriously addictive trap, whereby the search for the experience takes precedence over the experience itself (wanting becomes more important than liking). A game which handles this well would be "Robot Unicorn Attack". This game has no reward system; all the fun is derived from the pleasure of dashing (and then quickly exploding) through the rocks as a rainbow-trailing unicorn.

Games that require you to attend for more than an hour at a time. When you sit down to play a game, what is the shortest amount of time you need in order to make satisfying progress in the game? My rule of thumb is an hour; if you find that the structure of the game forces you to attend for longer than this, then I would suggest that this is unfairly making you overly dedicate time to the game. Normally, this is due to a social commitment that the game demands: group quests that require 4 hours to finish and which cannot be left without letting down your teammates are particularly cruel examples of this. A game which handles this well would be "Skyrim", in which you can save whenever you wish, meaning that you are never forced to play for long periods of time.

Games that have no end. Nearly every game that has been played addictively (rather than problematically) is laid out in such a way that the user never runs out of content. Within the gaming industry, the 'golden ticket' is to create a game that needs as little new content (graphics, animations, text and code) as possible for as much attendance as possible for the players. Ideally players will end up competing against or alongside each other and thereby find a never ending source of challenge. It is for this reason that online, social games are so much more addictive than offline ones. Games that have no end point (or an unreachable end point) can never be fully mastered and create an invitation to addiction, a process whereby the player sets their sights on claiming every prize the game has to offer, while the developers discretely work to ensure that this is never possible. A game that offers a satisfying end point at which players can happily disengage would include "The Last of Us".

Neuroscience and Neurobunk
A great deal of addiction studies, video game addiction included, are now relying heavily upon the field of

neuroscience to provide the answers. It is rare to read any article or paper on the subject without at least some recourse to what is going on in the brain during gaming. From this premise, games often receive criticism for unfairly manipulating us via our own internal chemistry.

This perspective considers the observable activity within the brain and is in contrast to much of what is presented in this book, which is focused on the thoughts and feelings of the gamer. As we move deeper into an era of increasingly disposable and high shock-value articles, it is important to be mindful of what you read and how you interpret the findings presented. While neuroscience has, and no doubt will continue to have, much to offer, its presentation in popular media needs to be treated with caution.

Brain studies in the field of video game addiction tend to focus on how dopamine, a natural stimulant in the brain, is ferried about during time spent playing. No decent discourse on the subject can ignore these findings – many of which need to be debunked and some of which can be pertinently inferred from. At the same time these findings are frequently taken as a springboard into describing games as being the cause of video game addiction. This is a non-scientific leap that risks overstating the role that video games play in video game addiction.

The focus of many such theories concern fMRI scanning (Functional Magnetic Resonance Imaging), which is, crudely put, a measure of blood flow around the different parts of the brain. It allows us to make correlations between activities. For example, we might notice that point A in the brain lights up when we look at our loved one as well as when we open a can of Coke.

Unfortunately this is where we cue the 'Neurobunk'. Respectable scientists and scientific journalists will treat these correlations as exactly that. That is to say that while they will notice a link between the two events, they will not go on to assume that one caused the other, or that the two are comparable in other respects. People who are looking to force a particular finding or get a top story may decide to overstate the link between two neuroscientific phenomena; in the above example, they might incorrectly deduce that we are in fact 'in love with cans of Coke' (or, equally logical, that we want to drink our loved one). This is precisely what The Sun did in 2014 when it claimed 'Gaming as addictive as heroin' (Parfitt 2014).

There was an interesting experiment carried out in 2006 in which the persuasive power of neuroscience was put to the test. Two sets of subjects were shown two sets of research papers. The papers were identical with the exception that one set used diagrams of the brain and the other did not, instead using other diagrams to convey its message. The result was that the people who had seen the brain diagrams were significantly more persuaded by the papers they had looked at than those that did not see the brain diagrams. The authors concluded that people were easily drawn in by the images of the brain as it supported the commonly held and comforting belief in reductionism – the idea that all activity in the universe, more specifically the mind, can be understood in terms of physical parts (McCabe & Castel 2006). It is from studies such as this that the 'put a brain on it' concept has come about; if you want to convince your audience then dazzle them with neuroscience. The aforementioned Sun article did exactly this by way of evidence.

Philosophically we are no closer to being able to bridge

the gap between what it is to think a thought or feel a feeling and the actual physical processes that happens in the brain. When I think of a sunset, no matter how far we have advanced in our understanding of the brain, no matter how much you dissect my 'grey matter', you will never find that sunset. The *qualia* – the individual internal experiences I have – cannot be described by any amount of physical 'stuff'.

Neuroscience is about looking at brain patterns on a sensory and motor level. While it is a practice that is used toward genuinely startling breakthroughs in our understanding of the brain, we must remember that philosophers and scientists continue to be stumped by the relationship between mind and brain (Bem 2006). Any attempt to link the two needs to be treated as the leap of faith that it is.

Neuro-babble such as 'engorges the nucleus accumbens' or 'overstimulated by your reward system' regularly emerges in online discussions and articles regarding video game addiction. Such phrases should always be read with caution, as should anything that includes the word 'neuroplasticity'. For those of you that are, like me, not neuroscientists, my advice would be to diligently check the sources to see if they are respected academically and that they are in fact the results reported. Otherwise, simply discount it. In addition, it bears remembering that in order to say anything meaningful about activity in the mind, brain activity needs to be compared across different activities and situations; more than one frame of reference is required. If we are to notice that dopamine is released during video gaming, then this can't simply be compared to one other activity – we need to understand it in the context of how dopamine release works across a broad spectrum of human activity as well considering its effect over time. If we are to say 'overstimulate' then we need to know what a normal level of 'stimulation' should look like.

Discussion: Does Gaming Cause Addiction by Releasing Dopamine in the Brain?

Video games have been subject to all manner of neuroscientific explanations. Many academics and science journalists seek to make use of neuroscience in order to 'dazzle' or even scare their audience into a distorted view of video games as more harmful than they are. Frequently, we are given comparisons between drugs and games, on account of them both releasing dopamine in the brain, a chemical that frequently correlates with a sense of euphoria and happiness (Sax 2009). From this position, some would seek to portray us as somehow chemically and deterministically dependent on gaming, once we've sampled it. One can imagine that a more impressionable reader might leave with the sudden terrifying revelation that games 'do something in your brain', as if that is a) scary and b) anything new. This is materialism gone mad, and a misuse of the advances we have made in neuroscience.

Things happen in our brain all the time. Not only that, but the release of dopamine is by no means restricted to game playing and crack addicts. Sex releases dopamine – while we know that some people become sex addicts, it would be a hard sell to convince anyone that sex 'caused' their addiction by releasing dopamine. Many, such as Sax – referenced above – suggest that video games are the *cause* of addiction by comparing the activity within the brain to that of a heroin user.

Our brains respond almost identically to heroin as they

do to an orgasm (Travis 2003); this does not tell us that sex is causing addiction; just that it, like games, like TV, can be misused. While heroin is also subject to abuse, it is important to remember that the scale of the chemical release in drug usage is huge in comparison to other activities, including gaming (Shaffer 2011).

A more accurate picture of dopamine is that it is more closely linked with 'wanting' rather than 'liking'. It itself is not figural in the more corporeal sensation that we think of when we imagine pleasure, rather it is more to do with the excitement we feel when we are anticipating pleasure (Berridge et al 2011). As we repeatedly take in the same stimuli, as is the case in addiction, we become tolerant. On a physical level, this is made clear by the fact that as an addict increasingly takes the same drug, the actual receptors in the brain that can encode the sensation as pleasurable become desensitized, effectively limiting future highs.

What doesn't get muted is the 'wanting'. No matter how immune we might become to a particular source of pleasure, we will continue to generate dopamine whenever we see cues in our environment that suggest that a 'hit' is close at hand. It is for this reason that recovering alcoholics will take very particular routes through town that will avoid all the pubs and bars; to be outside of one is to have their anticipation skyrocketing, even if the effect of the alcohol itself would be comparatively low.

Dopamine is a natural chemical that is bound up in all manner of addictions. Neuroscience sheds no further light than we already had in understanding that video games are one of many activities that have this effect. What it does tell us with more certainty is that while games can be a powerful trigger of dopamine release, they are not as severe as drug taking. Also, we can see that there is physical evidence for the possibility that video game addicts are actually caught in a cycle of expectation, whereby the thrill of anticipation is outperforming the diminishing sense of enjoying the experience of gaming itself.

Cause Four: The Decision to Escape

"I have absolutely no pleasure in the stimulants in which I sometimes so madly indulge. It has not been in the pursuit of pleasure that I have periled life and reputation and reason. It has been the desperate attempt to escape from torturing memories, from a sense of insupportable loneliness and a dread of some strange impending doom"
—Poe, 1848

In my clinical experience, the most frequent and significant cause and perpetuator of video game addiction is when someone's skills and ability to cope with their environment are overwhelmed and they are left feeling helpless, fearful or worthless. In short, this is the use of video games to combat fear and pain. Sometimes they are immediate and tangible, such as the presence of an abusive parent or chronic pain induced by a disease or impairment. In situations such as these, neither the game nor the gamer need addressing here, but the clearly untenable circumstances. More often games are used to cope with more elusive existential fears, such as the fear of being rejected, the fear of being alone or the fear of having to make decisions. When these existential fears coincide with someone who has a genuine interest and love of video gaming, then the invitation to addiction presents itself.

To a certain degree, gaming in order to cope with a distressing situation is a wise and healthy option and could be considered an act of self-care, much like having a single drink after a particularly stressful day at work. However, when addiction is present, players are facing deeper, more existential crises that are attacking the foundations of their self. It is when this coping strategy becomes regular and relied upon that the alarm bells should sound – when the signs of addiction are met and self-care has become self-harm.

In essence we are talking about escapism: using an activity to distract ourselves from other events. 'Escapism' is a term used in such a scattershot fashion that it has become near meaningless; it requires a little clarification before continuing, at least within this context. It seems that any hobby that offers immersion in a fictional or fantastical world can be classed as escapism, implying that no matter how powerful the story, how brilliant the game or how engrossing the film, participants will take part merely out of a desire to run away from something else. This is clearly not the case. Record-breaking numbers of cinema-goers did not flock to see the "Avengers Assemble" movie because they all wanted to 'escape' from their miserable lives – they did so because of the power and attractiveness of the Marvel superhero mythos.

Escapism refers to the urge to immerse into one world in order to avoid another. Games offer this like no other medium; titles like "Mass Effect" offer complex, elaborate and fascinating worlds that you can not only enter into, but also shape. It is not only the immersive qualities of a game that invite escapism. Nearly any game that offers a degree of challenge and difficulty will act as a powerful distraction from the world outside; the problem solving nature of gaming is such that it is very difficult to be simultaneously in touch with our physical and emotional feelings.

Gaming Addiction as a Commodity

Video gaming is perhaps the only product that actively promotes itself as being addictive, apart from Pringles, perhaps. It is difficult to envisage a bottle of beer sporting, '*Proven to cause alcoholism*' as a slogan, and yet frequently, game adverts will make claims such as 'the most addictive game ever'. This potentially dubious practice perhaps offers an insight in the nature of video gaming.

Unlike addictive substances, games sell themselves on immersion. Many players will deliberately look for titles that will lull them into playing for hours, tempting them to constantly go back to take on a new challenge or to simply wistfully lose themselves in the constant busywork that is offered to them. Roleplaying games such as the "Rift" and the "Fallout" series offer players the chance to sink deep into an alternative world that will, like our own life, offer up a 'to-do list' of activities. These activities will vary from the mundane tasks required for sustenance through to world-shaping quests in which the players take on the central role. While many gamers would balk at the prospect of knowingly losing hours in a game, there is a good proportion who are actively seeking to find a way to deliberately swallow up their lives. It would come as no surprise if many of these people are, potentially or actually, addicts.

It is perhaps a testament to the relative safety of games that they can afford to market themselves in this way. You can't have a bad trip on a game, catch an STD or be killed in a game. As discussed earlier, while there are a number of game-related deaths, these incidents are extraordinarily rare. On the whole, the selling point is that games offer an escape with no tangible risk. It may also be the case that the things that are risked by video game addiction – one's relationships, career and school work – are often the very things that addicts feel overwhelmed by and are looking to escape. When you are feeling hopeless about your social life, then an escape route that threatens to destroy said social life contains no real sting. It is important that gamers are given the right message. While gaming will not kill you nor irreparably damage you this does not make it a 'safe' addiction; what will suffer will be your relationships and self confidence, both of which will need time to heal once you get back in control of your gaming.

The existential fears that can drive us to hide in a world of gaming all have two unifying traits. Firstly, they are universal fears that we all have some experience of and secondly, they all, at their most terrifying, have the capacity to feel like a threat to our survival. This is much of the reason they are called existential fears – they describe and threaten what it is to exist. Each kind of existential fear threatens a different form of potential annihilation, be it death, overwhelming pain, loss of autonomy, rejection from society or paralysing indecisiveness.

When a gamer overuses the escapist quality of gaming in order to avoid these fears, then the game becomes about fighting for survival. It is for this reason that so many gamers find a creeping sense of *joylessness* in their gaming; the game is no longer about increasing happiness, it is now about staying alive.

In order to look at the different ways in which games can offer escapism from existential concerns, it is useful to think in terms of the different ways in which we experience the world. These can best be understood in terms of the physical world, the social world and the internal world of our thoughts and feelings (Binswanger 1946). This is a way of separating and looking at our experience that is used in psychotherapy. The two that are most relevant to video game addiction are those of the social and the internal worlds. Both of these correlate to a different aspect of our existence and both can prove so painful that we can opt for a flight into gaming. It is also worth noting that gaming can offer respite from physical distress – there are many chronic pain sufferers who use gaming to numb their discomfort. Sometimes, no doubt, this is to the point of addiction.

Escaping from the Social World

For some people being in the presence of others is problematic to the point of being terrifying, a difficulty recognised in psychiatry as social anxiety (American Psychiatric Association 2013). Relationships with others are inherently a stressful and fraught experience. While many of us become anxious and panicked about the prospect of delivering a presentation to our co-workers, some of us experience this level of negative emotion from simply going out with friends, holding a conversation at the bus stop or even leaving our front door.

Single-player games offer the absence of all relationships, and in this way they provide a direct head-in-the-sand effect for people that would like to shut out others altogether. While this is the route through which a portion of addicted gamers find themselves abusing games, addiction more often manifests through games that are played with others.

Increasingly, games are becoming a social experience. More and more games are played within an online community that generates its own hierarchy, scapegoats, rivalries, friendships and love interests. "World of Warcraft", "League of Legends" and "Planetside 2" are just a paltry few examples of the thousands of different games that now support their own network of players. Interestingly, as stated earlier, it is these types of online games that are most frequently played addictively.

While it might seem contradictory, players often gravitate to social online games in an effort to avoid the social world. Multi-player, online games allow players to converse within the confines of the game while avoiding face-to-face contact, thereby offering a more contained and safer social system. For many people there is discomfort and anxiety in having to deal with the complexities and vagaries of body language and facial expressions, as well as having to present your potentially unattractive physical self. For young people that are maturing into increasingly complex social situations, coming to terms with the fact that you simply don't know what others think of you is incredibly difficult. By not seeing the other and by not being seen, some gamers are able to maintain a social network while simultaneously negating the uncomfortable thoughts that they are, in some way, unworthy or unwanted. This concept, of the unsociable sociable gamer, is summed up in the notion of playing 'together alone' (Ducheneaut 2007). Players want the presence of others, but not the complication of face-to-face interaction. Sherry Turkle, in her investigation into how we increasingly use technology over each other, stated, "These days, insecure in our relationships and anxious about intimacy, we look to technology for ways to be in relationships and protect ourselves from them at the same time", (Turkle 2011).

In each of these games, communities are united by their avatars – their in-game personas. Consequently the power of their avatars, their equipment, their achievements and their ability to perform against the challenges of the game, are crucial marks of status that have an unavoidable influence on how and by whom you are accepted or rejected. This system of status is, by comparison to the subtleties of socializing, far simpler and obtainable. '*How do I get to level 80?*' is much more conceivable than '*How do I get people to laugh at my jokes?*' This process shows how video game addicts "slowly transfer this style of relating to objects to their interactions with people, treating them as one-dimensional objects to manipulate..." (Nakken 1996). Nakken was writing about addiction in general, but it isn't hard to see this process at work in gaming addiction where much of the appeal comes from the chance to reduce the chaos of the other into manageable, digital chunks.

Hence, many people who struggle to cope in the complex world of others will choose to hide in the more concrete and simplistic world of games. This behaviour often spirals into unmanageable levels of addiction by perpetuating itself in two powerful ways. The first is the inevitable vicious circle: as gamers become increasingly alienated from the outside world, they are increasingly driven into the game, which then further alienates them from the outside world, and so on. The second is when players find themselves running the risk of becoming inadequate *even in their gaming world*. For many players, especially in 24-hour, endless games such as most MMOs (Massive Multi-player Online) where the more time you invest, the more powerful you become; to not attend the game for any length of time is to fall behind. If I am in a group of roughly equal players and I am to take a two-week break due to a work commitment, I will run the risk that upon my return I will no longer be worth keeping in the group – they may even have gone to the extent of replacing me with someone else, someone that now outstrips my in-game power. This leads to an arduous and unenjoyable treadmill of 'keeping up with the Joneses'.

In this way, online gaming frequently leaves people feeling like they have no choice but to keep playing. Failure to keep up encourages a fundamentally terrifying thought: '*I couldn't make it out there, now I might not even make it in here*', leading to desperation to remain in the game as much as physically possible.

Many mobile games of today work on a very competitive level, "Clash of Clans" being a prime example. Games such as this require frequent checking in order to improve your performance against others. Some games even punish non-attendance, as per the appointment system mentioned in the introduction. When a player has reached a high position compared to others in a game such as this, it becomes mandatory for them to check as frequently as possible in order to maintain their standing. Not checking thereby leads to a creeping anxiety that they are sliding down the league tables and losing the social credit that they have worked so hard for in-game.

Many people who struggle in social situations will express their inadequacy as a disregard or even a dislike of others. This misanthropy, and arguably *all* misanthropy, is an interpretative shift that gamers make in order to preserve their self-worth. Typically, such people feel rejected by others on some level, or feel that if they are to enter into relations, they will ultimately become rejected. By deciding that others are in fact unworthy of their time, misanthropes find a way to explain their lack of intimacy and inclusion. Consider Aesop's fable of the fox and the grapes – in discovering that the lush-looking grapes were out of reach, the fox turns his nose up at them, declares them sour, and leaves (Asliman 2003).

I have worked with a number of young male gamers much like Aesop's fox. One particular young gaming addict described guys his own age as being 'cocky' and 'immature'. I suggested, after several months of counselling, that these generalizations might be actually saying something that he feared about himself instead. Saying that other guys were 'cocky' suddenly became 'I'm afraid I might not be man enough'; saying that they might be 'immature' became 'I think I'm boring to be around'. This kind of reframing had been crucial to keeping a crude but serviceable sense of dignity, and once the client saw the ruse for what it was, he described himself as feeling both vulnerable and alone. In the safety of counselling, we were able to take on these feelings and start to come up with some alternatives. Perhaps some guys were cocky and immature, and perhaps I don't come across as 'manly' and 'exciting', but perhaps that's ok. From here, the client started to lay down the games and take more social risks – he became more open to his fears. Acknowledgement brings control; for as long as we deny our negative feelings, they rule us from outside of our awareness.

Frequently people are faced with difficulties in their home life that they cannot think how to resolve. The head-in-the-sand nature of video gaming offers a quick route out of these extremely difficult and sometimes intimidating relationships. All of the addicted gamers I have worked with have reported at least one relationship in their household as being a lost cause. Sometimes it is a sibling, sometimes a spouse, often it is a parent. The gamer has, long ago, decided that they simply don't know how to reconcile or get along with the other person and has turned to video games. Ultimately, the gaming widens the gulf between those involved, leading the other to feel blanked and hurt, and the gamer to feel hopeless and alone.

Escape from the Internal World of Thoughts and Feelings

To be bored is to struggle with simply spending time with yourself. We all wrestle with the same fundamental concerns. We all find ourselves falling short of our own expectations leading to a sense of emptiness – an emptiness that manifests in existential fears such as death, chaos, meaninglessness, responsibility and other such inescapable truths (Yalom 1980). To be bored is to stand close to these painful realities of existence, something that few of us can bear and probably many of us can benefit from attempting more frequently. The fidgeting and restlessness with which we typically respond is our itching to get back to the distracting humdrum of living. Games, like work, like drama, like most hobbies, occupy the mind and distract it from the ghoulishness of being.

Many players will play because, *'there is nothing else to do'*. If they don't play, they run the risk of boredom. Some gamers I've worked with will astutely point out that to not play is to be faced with a world of thoughts that they openly admit as being distressing. To not game is to entertain deep and problematic questions such as, *'Am I making the most of myself?'*, *'Do I have enough friends?'*, *'Do*

I want to be in this relationship?', or '*What have I done that I'm proud of?*'

One of the most powerful and troubling thoughts that I have regularly encountered is, '*How can I prove myself?*' This is particularly the case with younger men I have worked with (the core demographic for video game addiction). It is about wanting to know that you have faced a challenge and overcome. Games offer this feeling to us in a powerful and direct way. Primarily they do this by providing a sense of constant measurable growth to the gamer: "League of Legends" sees you moving up through the league tables; "Temple Run" has you sporadically improving your distance, and all role-playing games and many others besides see your character inexorably gaining in level. This concrete and often numerical indication of progress can be hugely alluring to people who have no sense of how to develop or prove themselves away from games.

Gameplay typically works on loops of progress. These 'loops' involve a series of obtainable objectives that you complete in order to acquire the abilities, weapons, unlocks you need to open up a bigger, more difficult objective. With each new goal, you often attempt the same thing several times before you succeed and are then rewarded with the tools needed to attempt the next loop. In RPGs this is manifested in a constant drip-feeding of quests. Each one requires you to face a challenge, attempt (and typically re-attempt) until you succeed and then claim a reward. With each new quest, you get the sense that you faced a challenge, you overcame it, and now you have progressed.

Emmy Van Deurzen, in her book, *Everyday Mysteries*, talks of the dissociation that we have in modern culture between our work and the rewards we reap for our work.

Typically this manifests through the middle-man of money. As an adult, I understand that this plate of food I am eating, in this house, is a result of those potentially tedious years of work I've been dedicating to my employer; however this is a rational deduction that I have to make and not something that I can immediately appreciate on the level of gut feelings. As Van Deurzen points out, if we are to consider a far older, hunter-gatherer culture, we could quickly see that the connection between effort and reward is much more accessible. I am eating this dead deer on account of having just killed it. The link is more visceral and engaging. I did *that*, and got *this* (Van Deurzen 2009).

Particularly for the youth of today the link between effort and reward is highly obscure. What chance does a 14-year-old have of fully comprehending that this chronically dull algebra class will ultimately lead to a better standard of eating, leisure time, social status and housing conditions through a process of learning, examination, qualification, career and progression? Associating $3x$ to the power of $2y$ with the prospect of a financially comfortable retirement is neither intuitive nor obvious.

This disconnect between effort and reward contributes to many young people experiencing a sense of being useless or inadequate. People like to achieve through overcoming. While fleeting carrots such as "X Factor" and the chance to be a YouTube celebrity offer a chance for success, many young people are deeply affected by the prospect of *never making a difference*. Sometimes this is because they never get an opportunity. Sometimes it is due to poor education, poverty or social support. Other times it is because they are moving powerlessly on rails, albeit with a great deal of support, through a series of parental or educational expectations that they don't feel invested in.

Games offer challenge in abundance, as well as rewards for each challenge overcome. I kill this monster, I get this loot and experience. I find your lost amulet, you allow me into your city and so on and so on. Games also offer the chance to make a difference. This is typically done by saving the world, a task which, as a gamer, I have grown rather tired of doing. When it comes to gaming, the stakes are nearly always epically high; it's nearly always the world on the line and it's always only *you* that can save it. This caters to the innate fear of uselessness that all of us harbour; though games we have the chance to be the hero and make the ultimate difference.

Discussion: The Appeal of Failure

> *"For when all combine to make everything easier and easier, there remains only one possible danger, namely that the easiness might become so great that it would be too great; then only one want is left, though not yet a felt want – that people will want difficulty."*
>
> **—Kierkegaard, 1846**

It is interesting to note that one of the major appeals of hardcore gaming (and some casual games) is the chance of repeatedly *failing*. People who regularly game are typically setting themselves up to lose. This is particularly true in competitive multi-player games where inevitably someone has to. This has always been a large part of gaming's appeal – something that remains evident in today's abundant gaming market.

A fascinating study by Helsinki University investigated excitement levels in gamers. What they found was that players found more of a thrill in *nearly* succeeding (and thereby failing) than in succeeding (Ravaj 2006). An old wives' tale of game design is that players spend 80 percent of their time in the act of failing. Failure, it would seem, is popular. Many games market themselves on just how horribly difficult they are to get good at. Players will thrive on the fact that it is nigh on impossible to complete, that the competition is ridiculously high or that the nuances of the gameplay are so complex. "Dark Souls" and "Eve Online" are two of the many examples of games that have built cult followings in part due to their difficulty.

What if Kierkegaard, quoted above, is correct and we are now in an age of ease? He was quoted as saying this around 170 years ago; I suspect things are even easier in today's world. Scientific progress is largely about making things more accessible; in other words, making them easier to do. Travelling long distances, finding information, contacting friends, and taking medication are all made easier by science. Rarely does a breakthrough give us something new or banish something unwanted; most of the time it gives us more access to something we already have.

Gaming presents an academic problem that has been coined as the 'paradox of failure' (Juul 2013). Juul describes this as an extension of the age-old 'paradox of tragedy', both being situations in which humans actively seek out negative feelings through art, the former being failure, the latter misery. Juul describes humans as having an instinctive drive to seek out negative feelings in the world, but only in the long-term. On the immediate level, we will opt for success and happiness, but on a more unconscious level we recognise the importance of failure and opposition in the grand scheme of our lives and will seek out ways to include it.

Games provide surmountable opposition within a life where there is often little opposition, or where all opposition is easily surmountable. They may offer an oasis of difficulty in a desert of comfort and security. Many of the clients I have worked with, particularly young men, have considered themselves unsuitable for counselling as they have had no tragedy, no hardship and no opposition to overcome in their lives. I always point out that this is, in itself, a very precarious and paranoid place to find oneself; the fear of tragedy often looms larger when it has always been left to the imagination. Games, for these young men, frequently provide relief from their 'ideal' lives that they can end up relying on too much.

Over the last 10 years or so, interactive websites and mobile devices have increasingly become a part of my life. With this change has come my own struggle with the need to check in with social media, emails and most importantly, games. Something that I started to notice is an interesting correlation between my own doubts about what I am doing and the sudden need to check in on a game on my tablet. In the moment, I might experience a burst of interest to boot up a game and collect an appointment-based reward that might be waiting for me. On reflection, when I pause to consider, it becomes apparent that this urge often surfaces when I am in fact feeling lost or hopeless about my current project. Many times as I wrote this book I would go through the pattern of pausing, drawing a blank as to what to write next and then suddenly feeling inspired to check either Facebook or "Heroes of Dragonage" on my iPad Mini. Each time that I actually caught this behaviour, I was able to trace back, see past the apparent enthusiasm to check and instead notice the momentary hopelessness that I was looking to save myself from. In this way, checkable and portable gameplay offers a quick panacea to the internal difficulties that we run into; they consistently offer measurable progress where we feel we are making none.

Our internal world is a constantly churning and untameable sea of worry and questioning. For some of us, the ruminations that go through our minds in times of boredom, sleeplessness and reflection are too difficult to bear. I have mentioned some of the ways in which these thoughts can become frightening and unbearable, but there are others. Some of us frequently obsess over work, some of us are constantly perplexed by our inevitable deaths and some of us are deeply ill at ease with the body, sexuality, gender or role that we feel we have been assigned by our culture. Video gaming enables us to switch off from these transmissions. For some of us, the need to drown out our reflective monologue becomes an obsession and this, in turn, leads to addiction.

Zinberg's Drug, Set and Setting

Norman Zinberg, an American psychoanalyst and psychiatrist, contributed to the field of drug and alcohol treatment with his 'drug, set and setting' model. This described how the effects of any given drug were made up of three parts: the **drug** itself, the mind**set** and nature of the user as well as the **setting** (or situation) in which the user took the drug (Zinberg 1986). Zinberg's model was originally engineered to help understand people's response to substances, but offers a useful paradigm around which we can bring together our thoughts on what leads someone to become addicted to video games.

Firstly, the **drug** itself had some influence. Caffeine, for example, is likely to cause increased alertness and locomotion, cannabis is likely to do the reverse, and so on. In the instance of video games, we therefore need to acknowledge the potential that video games have for being used as a crux for addiction. It is also important to note how some games are more likely to be used this way than others: specifically online games and, more specifically, role-playing, first-person and real-time strategy games.

Secondly was the **set**, which referred to the mindset of the user; here Zinberg highlights how different drugs will work differently for different people. Firstly, the demographic of an individual is important here – we know that those who are most vulnerable to addictive video gaming are typically going to be young men. However, Zinberg was referring to more than just inherent makeup. He also includes a person's attitudes, behaviours and beliefs as being part of the 'set' of the user. From what we know, we can say that an addicted video gamer is likely to struggle socially, is unlikely to have many long-term plans for themselves and is likely to spend much of their time wrapped up in their own thoughts. Additionally, it is frequently the case that the gamer, prior to the gaming becoming an addiction, was struggling with either a sense of powerlessness or hopelessness, either in their relationships with others or their own sense of self.

Finally, Zinberg recognises the importance of the **setting** – the environment. Where and how we expose ourselves to potentially addictive behaviours has a huge impact on how we respond to them. As mentioned before, the one setting that seems to be a breeding ground for video game addiction is when one of the gamers is at odds with someone else in the household. Freedom to access video games away from other members of the household at any time of day or night is also another regular aspect of the environment for problematic video gamers, a freedom that should be used with caution. The accessibility of gaming is crucial to the setting. The more we can get to the game, either though being off work with nothing else to do, or by having the game on our phone in our pocket 24/7, the more we are likely to become addicted.

We need to be careful with any belief regarding the cause of video game addiction, particularly where we are personally affected. The likelihood is that we are out to blame someone. Zinberg gives equal weight to the behaviour used, the user and the situation in which that person is making the choice to use. In this way he distributes the cause across a range of factors, giving a more holistic and more realistic picture. This information should serve to help us notice early on when video gaming addiction is a risk, to take steps to avert it before it becomes a reality, and finally to provide insight and understanding as to how the problem came about. At the same time, one should always be mindful that these indicators are a guide. If you want to know if someone is an addict do not use stereotyping or demographics to give you an answer: that is discrimination. Check their behaviour and thoughts against the six signs, as laid out in chapter two.

CHAPTER FOUR

Resolving Video Game Addiction

What follows is a structured collection of some of the best approaches to tackling the problem of gaming addiction. As with the methods of measuring video game addiction, much of what is written here has been handed down to us from the world of substance abuse. Because of the important differences between these issues some practices are omitted, others have been added in.

This section presents 10 separate steps that can be used depending on the needs and situation of each individual. At the end are two smaller sections providing more specific information and advice to both the loved ones and health professionals, as well as a brief consideration for people working in the games industry who are keen to make games that ethically bear in mind the medium's potential for misuse.

There are effectively two paths of progress that are being followed simultaneously in order to affect recovery. The first is to increase the gamer's awareness of their thoughts and feelings (both when gaming and when away from gaming); the second is to begin gradually controlling how they play video games.

People who are addicted will typically have a host of thoughts and feelings that they are in the constant business of burying. These 'horrors', as Poe called them (albeit in relation to drinking), become increasingly terrifying the more that they are kept at bay. Much like a phobia, the more that we successfully avoid the object of our fears, the more we reinforce that the object of our fears needs to be avoided. It is by experiencing or confronting the feared outcome that we establish a more controlled and rational relationship to it.

Gamers that are hiding away from fearful aspects of their lives can often make use of counselling to come to a more informed decision about how they deal with them. The support of friends and family is also invaluable in this regard and counselling should ideally be a supplement rather than a substitute for this. Recognition of the misery or anxiety that drives people to game is no guarantee that they will then stop misusing gaming. A 14-year-old living powerlessly in a house of marital violence and abuse may come to terms with his situation and decide that, '*Yes, being lost in video games is preferable – there's nothing I can do to change the situation*'. For the most part, however, new options are available. The gamer should lead the way once they have been challenged with the reality of their feelings.

There is a common trap here that households should remain vigilant of: scapegoating. In domestic situations that are unpleasant to the degree that a person has elected to hide away in gaming, other family members might begin to prey on the gamer and their habit as being 'the problem'. This can easily escalate to the point where the original problems in the house begin to diminish as the non-gamers increasingly come together in adversity against the common enemy of video games. In this situation, the entire household is invested in the addicted gaming of the silently elected scapegoat; on some level they know that to remove it will quickly lead to an unravelling that may well end up implicating them.

Families that hold up addicted gaming as the single, biggest problem in the household should consider carefully what it was like before that came along and what they *really* envision life would be like without this problem. There is the possibility that the gamer is effectively 'taking one for the team'. In such situations, couple or family counselling is essential, in addition to any counselling being provided to the gamer on an individual basis.

Where the issue is not one for family counselling the gamer needs to come to terms with their buried fears. Short-term work needs to be done to reduce or control the gaming, even if it is only marginally and for brief periods. While the addiction is in full swing it is difficult for anyone, even a counsellor, to break into the bubble of the gamer's world as the behaviour keeps the defences well maintained. Once the space is made, then the otherwise repelled feelings can be brought into focus. While this process is often profoundly challenging and should be undertaken in a safe way, people will typically find that they have far more resilience and ability to cope with their situation than they had expected. The crutch of the game had made them forget the strength they actually had.

At the same time, by enabling a gradual sense of control over our thoughts and feelings, a gamer's sense that they no longer need to rely upon the addiction will be instated. The more the gamer gains a sense of emotional control, the less they will need the games. The less they use the games, the more control they will gain over their emotions. This cycle generally starts off in reverse, as a vicious circle: '*I cannot gain in emotional strength because I spend all my time hiding in games, and I cannot reduce the amount of time I spend gaming because I have no emotional strength to deal with what it would bring up for me*'. It is down to all involved to reframe this cycle into being both virtuous and self-fulfilling.

The 10 Steps

Each of the steps should be considered by all involved: the gamer themselves, their loved ones and finally, any professionals working with the gamer. While some steps are exclusively for the gamer to carry out themselves, many of them require input from several parties. All of them need as much support as can be offered to the gamer.

1. **Adopt an Attitude for Recovery**
2. **Take a Tech Detox**
3. **Arrange Offline Activities**
4. **Begin Gaming Mindfully**
5. **Draw up Boundaries**
6. **Maintain Boundaries**
7. **Seek Professional Help**
8. **Go Public**
9. **Reach out to Others**
10. **Review**

The steps shown here are primarily designed for gamers that are addicted. At the same time it can be hard to decide whether someone has a gaming addiction (showing all the signs of addiction), or if they are merely playing problematically (showing some of the signs of addiction). In most cases, the best thing to do will be to work through the steps incrementally and see if the problem starts to reduce. For most problematic gamers, things should start to improve after the first four, or in more acute situations, the first six. If the gaming persists in being a problem and the first six steps are not making a difference then you are most likely looking at addiction, in which case implement seven to nine, with 10 (reviewing) being done every three months after that. As you progress through the steps, work to keep each of the previous ones in place. As successes happen at later stages, it will often provide more support to the gamer's efforts to affect the earlier, more difficult stages.

Ultimately this is a pragmatic and measurable system being applied to a very messy and human process. Consequently, do not feel defeated when things don't 'fit'. From having worked with gaming addiction I can tell you that they never do, at least not in any tidy way. What you will most likely find is that as you continue to make efforts in one direction, another direction will suddenly improve. For example, you might implement a tech detox for you and your gamer addict wife (step two) that she fails to stick to. Rather than becoming demoralised, you should remain aware of how this might have had unseen benefits, such as her suddenly having a more honest attitude to the fact that she has a problem (step one). There will be steps that don't seem to work or are too difficult to implement given the current mindset of the gamer. Often the best solution is to try another step. Once you have some movement elsewhere, revisit the one that was initially difficult.

Step 1: Adopt an Attitude for Recovery

"Insanity: doing the same thing again and again and expecting different results".
                    —Albert Einstein (reputedly)

The first crucial step, as with any addiction, is to acknowledge that there is a problem. The gamer needs to admit that their current plan for managing life is not working, not for themselves or those around them. This stage, while possible to achieve without support, often requires the input of loved ones in order for the gamer to appreciate how important it is that they change.

Addicted gamers, as with substances abusers, are likely to have built up an image of themselves as being successfully in control of their behaviour; convinced that it is not nearly as problematic as others perhaps make out. We all have the ability to adapt our interpretations of the world in order to best fit the self-image that we want to cultivate. If I am wholeheartedly committed to understanding myself as a conscientious gamer, then I will need some radical reinterpreting in order to hold on to this self-image when I miss work in favour of spending the day on "World of Warcraft". I might say that I didn't really want the job, that I'm owed time off or that I'll work overtime to make up for it at a later date. All of these would be tricks of the mind to avoid the realisation that my gaming has started to take over my life and that I need to make a change.

Some addicted gamers will reluctantly attend counselling, training or motivational interviewing without any real acceptance of the harm their hobby is creating. They will often be protective of their gaming being taken away by people that they see as allied with the significant others who have strong-armed them into attending. This situation rarely has a directly positive impact, although in the long run it can help build a picture for the gamer until they admit that there is a serious problem. Sometimes they are kick-started into realisation when they come to understand that if they don't get in control of their gaming, they may risk having to give it up altogether. Other times they will acknowledge unhappiness before they admit the gaming as a problem; a recognition that can provide professionals a way into working with them.

The Recovery Message
In order to set the gamer in a positive direction such that they can best benefit from the following process, they need to begin by embracing what I call the recovery message: a relatively simple series of statements that provide an overview of the entire process of recovery.

My gaming has become a problem that is affecting both me and those around me. What I've been doing so far to control it has not worked. I need to make a radical change in my behaviour in a way that I have not tried before.

Through the course of regaining control, the gamer will need to revisit this statement and come to learn each part of it experientially – that is, out there in the world of others, not just on paper. Below are approximations of the standpoints that need to be adopted. These are there to be played with – some factors may not be relevant, some others may need to be added in. All of them should be reworked to fit the nature of the gamer's situation, while keeping their essence intact:

My gaming has become a problem that is affecting both me and those around me. *This situation has become untenable. I am suffering because I am focusing my life around my gaming habits. I am holding myself back from achieving, from socialising, from being healthy, from my family and most importantly I'm still left unhappy and unfulfilled. Others who care for me are also suffering, either through my irritability when they obstruct my gaming or through the rejection I leave them with by valuing gaming over spending time with them.*

What I've been doing so far to control it has not worked. *The attempts I have made to control my gaming haven't worked whatever they may be. I cannot hope to attempt them again and achieve a success, nor can I hope to just 'try harder' with any of them. Any attempt to change this pattern that contains the same behaviours as a previous attempt is likely to fail.*

I need to make a radical change in my behaviour in a way that I have not tried before. *I have to make one or a number of concrete changes in my behaviour, be that attending counselling, moving my PC into the lounge, taking up another hobby, ditching the games, etc. The important point is that I have to act in a different way to how I have acted previously. If that change doesn't work, I need to make another. Each change must be substantial, behavioural, discussed with others and carried out wholeheartedly.*

In order to use the recovery message effectively, the gamer should meet with others in their household, read through it and then have an open conversation as to how much they feel they can relate to it. If they take it on board then they should back this up by either saying it to the others in the house or writing it down for others to see. They key is to own it, and this is best done by hearing it said in the presence of others or committing it to paper.

For those for whom it sits with more uncomfortably, they should decide what they can agree with, what they want to alter and what they would like to remove. Once they have done this, they can then speak out about what remains. It is vital that they only use the parts that they feel they can apply to themselves. It is equally important that they revisit it and amend it as their recovery progresses.

It may be the case that this is too hard a concept for them to buy into immediately and other steps need to happen first. Even in these instances, by making it clear at the outset that an internal shift in attitude is primary to starting any significant change, you prime the addict toward recovering. As other steps are taken and more acknowledgements are created in the gamer they will be able to revisit the message and own it more for themselves.

In speaking this message, the gamer is having to begin the process of rewiring deeply ingrained habits. To directly change addictive behaviours is to try and alter these powerful and chemically reinforced habits. Our brains are like a woodland of different possibilities; the more we repeat our route through the same set of choices, the more we cut a new and specific path through the undergrowth. These paths become habits; they are easy to walk down, following any little-used alternative results in battling through a sea of weeds and bushes. For a fuller explanation of this, see Duhig's recent and excellent book on habits (Duhig 2011). Habits fool us into thinking that they are an essential part of ourselves, creating a crisis of identity when we consider breaking out of them. In this way, a gamer can come to see themselves as being defined by gaming. The prospect of removing it can lead to a panic as to who they would 'be' should they not be a gamer. Phrases such as, '*It's just what I do*', or '*That's the way I am*', are typical indicators of this kind of existential fear being associated with the cessation of gaming.

Jesse Schell, a game designer, brilliantly stated, "We become what we pretend to be" (Schell 2008). Closely linked to the process of habit formation is our ability to mimic the behaviours of a desired persona and, before long, find ourselves *being* that persona. Recent studies led by Amy Cuddy have shown that this is even true on a chemical level – act a certain way and your body will chemically morph to match and reinforce the behaviour (Cuddy 2012).

People whose gaming habits have progressed to the point of addiction are going to need to give up their sense of self in order to make headway. If their behaviours go a long way to describing who they are, and their current behaviours are not acceptable, then they need to be prepared to *not feel like themselves* in order to change. Maxwell Maltz, a plastic surgeon turned psychologist writing in the '60s, said that, "Our self-image and our habits tend to go together. Change one and you will automatically change the other" (Maltz 1960).

In situations where the gamer simply cannot identify with the recovery message it is best to consider the problem a household issue rather than trying to force the issue onto them. In these instances family counselling is by far the best option.

In order to break out of the habits that they have formed, addicted gamers need to let go of any rigid view of who they are. They need to appreciate the malleability of the human soul; without this acceptance, change becomes far harder. By being able to say and own the recovery message they have gone a long way to achieving this.

2. Take a Tech Detox

Something that is frequently incorporated into internet addiction treatment is a period of complete abstinence from any kind of technology, typically a 72-hour tech detox. This means three straight days of no phones, tablets, laptops and television. For someone addicted to games, this is short enough to be a realistic and feasible request (though it certainly won't feel so to them, at least at the outset) and long enough such that they will be forced to be creative in finding new ways to occupy themselves.

The whole household should support the gamer by taking part in the detox alongside the gamer; they will undoubtedly benefit from doing so. Our modern lifestyles trick us into feeling that we have reliance upon technology. Breaking this illusion reignites an empowering sense of control and creativity in the majority of people that undertake such a detox. If one or several members of the household fret that they can't do this, then they are modelling the very same behaviour that you are looking to resolve, all the more reason for them to show real support by doing the hard thing and putting the devices aside.

Such a jarring break from up to 10 or more hours a day of gaming can potentially leave the gamer in a difficult and untenable position. It is important to mitigate this by making sure that the three days are filled with other distractions. Ideally this could be an activity-packed holiday or excursion but could equally involve the household embarking on a series of three day-trips or micro-adventures. There are certain types of activity that are more beneficial than others in this situation, as I will discuss next. The tech detox serves as an important springboard into more boundary-driven behaviours (boundaries will be discussed more later), marking a turning point after which the gamer will be better able to stick to rules around how much they should use games within their lives.

This step can be a useful litmus test as to whether or not addiction is present. If the supposedly addicted gamer engages with relatively little conflict then it is perhaps a sign that they are not addicted. In these instances it is then worth asking whether they are merely a problematic gamer or if they have been simply really enjoying gaming. Additionally, as a standalone exercise, the tech detox can be a great way for a household to assess its reliance on screens and reconnect.

3. Arrange Offline Activities
The gamer will need to re-establish relationships with both others and themselves. The former will happen by creating time for face-to-face relationships, the second by allowing the gamer to regain a sense of their own bodies. Both of these can be quickly achieved through activities that focus on physicality and teamwork. Such activities can rarely be done in isolation. Consequently having people about to help coordinate and arrange such endeavours is often valuable if not crucial.

These kinds of activities are much of the focus of treatment centres such as the Smith & Jones clinic in

Amsterdam and the South Korean boot camps; aerobics on the beach, long walks and sports are all par for the course. Getting gamers to embark on such AFK ('away from keyboard') ventures is the hard part. Once they have started to do so, it is normally relatively quickly that they start to discover new sources of enjoyment and pleasure.

As with the tech detox and counselling, the entire household should support these activities through getting involved themselves. If you are a couple, book a weekend camping; if you are in a larger family, perhaps organise a day of hiking. The possibilities are endless, though typical choices would be: indoor skiing/rock climbing, cycle rides, go-karting, paintballing, tennis, miniature golf and the like. Wherever possible keep the emphasis on physical movement and communication.

Being in and amongst nature can be hugely curative in these situations. Many of us live in highly urbanised and digitized environments that are designed to meet our needs and see that we are able to go about our lives without hindrance. Nature is not so kindly constructed, presenting fallen trees to hop over, brambles to pick one's way past and steep hills to climb. All of this serves to give us a connection to our world and, more importantly, our bodies. This kind of connection to our physicality becomes dulled during prolonged periods in front of a screen. Going for a walk, a camping trip or an off-road cycle creates a sense of physical purpose and accomplishment that is needed in order to offer an alternative at a time when a distraction from video gaming is sorely needed. The real challenge is to encourage the gamer to venture outside. Often the very prospect of a challenge will be what entices them to take part.

With all activities away from gaming, be conscious of the availability of games on different devices. A typically addicted gamer will settle for a game on their smartphone if they are denied access to their console, even if the experience is a lower standard. As a result, if you are to detox, go hiking or spend time together, be conscious that access to mobiles might well undermine the process.

This step is a natural progression of the tech detox, for which you will need offline activities in order to make it work. Like the previous step, even the mildest of problematic gamers can greatly benefit from it. Investigating other options away from screens can be broadening for many of us given the ubiquity of technology.

4. Begin Gaming Mindfully

The gamer, now aware of their predicament, needs to now return to their hobby in an entirely new and more mindful fashion. The goal here is to encourage play in a conscious and present way, rather than them losing themselves into the game, ignoring the passing of time and shutting out both their bodily needs as well as their own emotional awareness.

The gamer should start a diary or log sheet, one that works around the needs and lifestyle of the gamer. Keep track of at least two things: firstly, the time spent playing in a day and secondly, the approximate emotional wellbeing. This is effectively asking, '*When did you game and what was it like?*'

The latter is best monitored on a scale of 1-to-10, being recorded after each hour of gaming or each visit to a mobile or browser game. A 1 would represent a terrible session of gaming, one in which the player felt powerfully

depressed or angry and with little enjoyment of the game;
A 10 would mean that they had a positive mood, loved
the game and felt great for playing it. Ultimately, you
want a measure of how enjoyable any given hour of
gaming was. Below is an example of a log sheet that has
been filled out. The final column offers a brief place for
the gamer to notice anything particular about their
sessions of gaming. An empty version of the log sheet can
be found at the back of the book.

An Example Gaming Log Sheet

MONDAY		
Hours of Gaming	**Enjoyment**	**Comments**
10–11am	9	*Started playing a new game*
11–12am	5	
1–2pm	6	*just argued with _____ at lunch*
2–3pm	3	
11–12pm	2	*Only about 20min before I went to bed. Waste of time.*

Total Time Gaming Today: *5 hours*

This is adapted from a method put forward by Alex
Blaszczynski (1998) for problem gambling, in which users
would log the time spent gambling. With both gambling
and gaming, the effect is the same, in that quite quickly
the player will become surprised at how much they game,
worried by how wrong they were in their estimations and
hopefully become more aware of the passage of time in
their future sessions. Logging the level of enjoyment

during each session should begin to make the gamer aware of the powerful paradox at the heart of their gaming – that despite their initial response to games being positive and enjoyable, the majority of their interactions have now become empty and numb.

Depending on the level of self-reflection in gamers, this process of diary keeping will have one of two outcomes. Many players will balk once they realise exactly how much time they are committing to an activity that isn't providing a great deal of pleasure and set about making a change. Other, more reflective players, may brush this information aside, arguing that 'numb' is exactly what they were aiming for – this is often the case for players that are aware of their desire to escape from life. Some people who readily identify their lives as miserable may make the informed decision that continuing to overuse gaming is a better option than facing the world. However, even in such instances, they will at least go back to doing so mindfully, which will undoubtedly lead to a more measured and deliberate approach.

Another potentially powerful effect of the diary is that it often will start to reveal patterns. If the gamer begins to make use of the diary regularly, they can begin to develop it by recording key events each day. These events can build up a description of triggers, pointing to circumstances and incidents that are most likely to send them into a binge of play. When shared with a counsellor or psychotherapist, these triggers can provide information about the difficulties in someone's life that are typically buried beneath gaming.

To assist in timekeeping ensure that a large and clear clock is always next to the gaming monitor. This is good practice for any gamer, even if they are not keeping a diary. Being unaware of the passage of time is a problem for some gamers even if they don't game to problematic levels. The clock and the diary together will begin to make the gamer more present in the act of gaming, making it harder for them to become lost in the repetitive cycles of play.

Monitoring time spent gaming is an increasingly difficult task these days as gaming has become so granular and intrusive with casual gaming. I play "Words with Friends", and am dimly aware how that game can quietly eat up over an hour of my day in tiny, transitional chunks – each imperceptibly slipped in between the day's tasks. A quick word while I shuffle to the bathroom, a brief scan of my options while I wait (longer than I need to, frequently) for a download and so on. Where there is the possibility of addiction it is important, perhaps by use of a stopwatch, to keep a track of all these tiny spots of gaming. Individually they are insignificant, but together they can contribute to unhealthy gaming whilst maintaining their guise of insignificance. For someone that games in these tiny, snack-able chunks, the following process can help create an awareness of the time they are spending:

1. Use a stopwatch to time how long they spend during each visit to a game. Ideally do this throughout a single typical day.
2. From this, work out the average length of a visit.
3. From now on, use the log sheet or diary to mark down each time they check in or play as a tally.
4. At the end of each day, use the tally to work out the time spent in short visits.
5. Make sure to add this to the time spent in any longer, more substantial sessions.

Getting to a point of being aware of how much you are investing in gaming can take time but is essential. Without a clear idea of the impact on the day the problem is too easy to brush under the carpet. Anybody with a gaming problem, not just addicts, should work toward this level of awareness. All the steps up to this point (one through four) form a useful suite of behaviours for problematic gamers beyond which they may not need to progress. If performing these has had no substantial impact, then move onto numbers five and six.

5. Draw Up Boundaries

From here, a new set of boundaries will need to be decided upon. While the goal here is in part to try to limit the amount of time that the gamer spends gaming, it has a more important aim of getting them to be in control of their gaming.

Boundaries, in this case, refer to agreed limitations on the amount of time someone spends gaming. For example, this might mean limiting gameplay to no more than one hour a day or only making sure that all devices are switched off between 10 p.m. and 10 a.m. Understanding and effectively implementing boundaries is the hard work of responding to an addiction; someone who finds themselves addicted is, almost by definition, someone that is struggling with boundaries. Their life has become enmeshed and chaotic. Such a person will likely need some support and education to come to terms with the importance of boundaries and, most importantly, how to best maintain them.

Drawing up a system of boundaries should be a collaborative process between the gamer, their household and any professionals working with them. The more involvement that the gamer has, the more invested they will be in maintaining them. If they are left out of the decision making process, then they are much less likely to keep to them. Equally, if the gamer draws up boundaries on his own, he only has himself to answer to, which is likely to fail. The more people around the gamer that are aware of the new rules that have been drawn up, the more the issue is out in the open and the more help the gamer can get in keeping to the system.

It is worth investigating the game or gaming device that is most commonly being used to see if it has a parental control feature that allows you to set limits for how much it can be played in a given time frame. All major consoles contain this feature, as does Blizzard's "World of Warcraft". If you do use this feature, make sure it doesn't lead to complacency; be aware of the gamer merely switching to another game when their time allocation is used up. Nonetheless, these systems are an encouraging sign that developers are becoming mindful of their users and can be a great asset in helping those addicted to gaming.

Well-designed boundaries will have the following qualities:

1. **Acceptability**. The boundaries should be chosen in such a way that all involved will be happy if they are stuck to. Don't choose a system that ends up enabling more play than people are comfortable with; be sure that if the gamer plays as much as possible within the limits, everyone involved can be satisfied that the result is an improvement.

2. **Specificity**. Only deal in concrete, measurable limits. Only being able to play before 10 p.m. could lead to

difficulties when someone is playing at 4 a.m. in the morning (*'Is this before the deadline or after?'*). Each boundary must be without ambiguity.

3. **Simplicity**. Don't come up with some elaborate system that takes into account lots of eventualities and contingencies. The complexity will create confusion and this will make the boundaries harder to police and easier to wriggle out of.

4. **Realism**. The goal is not to eradicate or minimize gaming; it is to bring about a level of control. Allow some generosity into the system, such that the gamer will, without doubt, get a good crack of the whip each week when they play. If someone has been playing for 60 hours a week and then adheres to boundaries only allowing them 30, then this has gone a long way to creating control, even though the time spent gaming is still considerable.

5. **Consideration**. Different games require different patterns of play. RPGs that involve group quests will often require a significant time investment. A system of boundaries that only allowed an hour a day would severely limit a gamer's ability to enjoy such games; no play on weeknights, on the other hand, would still enable them to take part in substantial gaming sessions on the weekend. Take these patterns of play into account when drawing up the system.

You can afford to be creative in deciding how much gaming is acceptable and under what circumstances. There are many, many different ways of putting together a system of boundaries and it should come down to what is right for your situation. As a springboard to your coming up with boundaries, here a few different examples of boundary systems:

- All 'tech' is off between 10 a.m. and 8 a.m. on weekdays
- You have 10 hours gaming to spend a week, however you want
- No gaming on weekdays
- You can game for up to two hours a day, no more
- You can have the tablet every other day
- You get to spend one hour gaming for each hour studying (credit system)

The last is an example of a 'credit system'. This is perhaps the system of choice for the desperate, hair-losing parent of obsessive gamers. In short, credit systems involves the parents and child (assuming that the child is the gamer) agreeing that gaming time can be 'bought' through other means, be it time away from the games, chores, homework, socialising or whatever avenue the parent feels there is a deficit in.

In my experience and in reviewing the literature around gaming addiction, credit systems like this often, though not always, fail. Consequently they should be approached with caution as, by making gaming a reward, its salience can increase such that the gamer ends up continuing to orientate their life around it. You are effectively describing gaming as a goal, which makes it more coveted thereby promoting wanting over liking. Consider other options before trying a credit system.

6. Maintain Boundaries

Once in place, the hard work begins. For the gamer, this means having to restrain themselves from their instinctive responses when faced with boredom, upset, pain and any other difficulties that they otherwise might face. For the parents of gamers, this is going to involve policing and enforcing boundaries in the face of their child's disapproval. Finally, for partners, friends and spouses, it will require them to equally risk their relationship with the gamer by enforcing boundaries but without the authority of being a parent. In these situations, encouragement and honesty become all the more important.

In order to make boundaries work as well as possible the gamer should try some of the following self-control practices:

- **Delay Starting**: Each time the gamer goes to play, they note down the time and wait. After a few minutes, they go ahead and play. The goal is to increase this period of time, not to the point where gaming doesn't happen, but such that the gamer can prove to themselves that this is something they have control over. Start off with a minute, and then gradually work up to 10 minutes. After that, they might see how long they can go. Over time, the sense of *having* to start gaming will be replaced by a choice.

- **Finish Early**: Much as with the above, this can increase a sense of control over the game play, reducing the belief that the player needs to extract every last drop of 'fun' out of time spent gaming. It also works to reduce the sense of being wrenched away to another activity; if a gamer plays up to the last second before having to go to school, they will go through the rest of the day with the sense of being 'incomplete' until they can get back to the game. By enforcing a cooling-off period between finishing gaming and other activities the game can become something that happens in amongst life, rather than vice versa.

- **Change Games**: Some games are more geared toward being played addictively than others. Mobile, appointment-based games are focused on getting players to check in frequently, punishing them if they fail to do so and MMOs frequently leave offline players feeling like they are missing out. Sometimes the only way to make boundaries achievable is to change games. This can be a hard pill to swallow, but in some instances particular players are not cut out for particular games and are doomed to overcommit. However, if the gamer does change games, encourage them to take the time to say goodbye to any gaming community they have become part of – they will doubtless support the gamer and understand.

- **Avoid Substitutes**: There is nothing more tantalizing to a gamer than watching videos of their favourite games. They serve to ramp up the feelings of wanting without ever dispelling the illusion. As is the peculiar nature of anticipation, even though gamers would nearly always take gaming over watching gaming, it is typically *far* more fun to do the latter. Non-gaming media about gaming whips people up into a state of expectancy. If a gamer is in the process of cutting back, sources such as YouTube gaming channels, gaming-related forums, magazines, blogs or TV shows need to be either ruled out or considered 'gaming time' for purposes of keeping boundaries. If it is not controlled the gamer will use it to end up obsessing all the more.

Recognising and Dealing with Resistance

Once boundaries have been established, it is inevitable that the part of the gamer that craves time spent playing will unconsciously seek to try and re-assert itself. Firstly, this is because that gamer is habitually hard-wired toward gaming on an instinctual level. Secondly, in stopping or limiting the amount of gaming, you are effectively cutting off a coping strategy from the gamer, one that they will naturally want to turn to.

Over time, these strategies and habits will be replaced by new ones and things will become easier. However, at least initially, the addicted gamer, and those around them, will need to be vigilant for signs of a return to old patterns and behaviours, as there are myriad devious and ingenious ways in which a craving mind will go about manipulating situations back into feeding its desires.

What follows are some of the more frequent sabotaging thoughts that gamers will have when they are struggling to control their gaming. Each is written as it would be heard internally (and frequently externally when arguing with others). Each comes with a response – this provides the self-talk that the gamer should employ to help themselves keep or regain control. Equally, the response can be used by those supporting the gamer in order to highlight and undermine the sabotaging thoughts compelling them toward breaking boundaries.

Certainly, any addicted gamer looking to stick to new boundaries should go through the following list. Once they start to know what thoughts to look out for, the process become easier to notice and inhibit. They are as follows:

'I'll only go a few minutes over'

If you need to stop by 6 p.m. then stop *before* 6 p.m. Once boundaries are in place they need to be monitored strictly. When a behaviour unconsciously attempts to exert its influence, it will do so by making boundaries indistinct. Therefore, they need to remain rock solid. Even going up until the minute hand is 'roughly' at 6 p.m. should be considered a failure. You need to stop by 6, after two hours, when your husband gets home or whenever you have agreed.

Response: Boundaries are not targets; they are there for you to practice control. Don't leave the clock to make the final decision for you. Flex your mental muscles by pulling the plug in advance.

'Just one more go'

Classic and time-honoured in gaming, the one-more-go mentality has made Rovio's "Angry Birds" a money-making giant. Many games are designed to make the player feel as if success lies just around the corner. This is achieved through bite-sized gaming sessions, a constant gentle increase in player learning and random events that *might just* cause you to get lucky in any given attempt.

The temptation is to think that you will do better on your next go. The trap is that if you *do* better, then you will want to keep playing *even more*. The idea that you will somehow be more inclined to finish gaming after another attempt is a self-created illusion. Stop now, as one more go is not an option.

Response: You can have another go, but when you are next allocated time for gaming, you can't go past your boundaries.

'I've had a hard day'
Addicted gamers that have had to reduce their gaming are going to have a series of bad days, in fact, as the conflict sign of addiction shows us, you are likely to be aggressive, irritable and generally stroppy with everyone and anyone. Arnold Washton describes addiction as an attempt to live an idealised life in which nothing can go wrong (Washton 1989). Consequently, any attempt to limit the behaviour *should* feel tough, as the gamer has to face a more real and initially more uncomfortable world.

Do not turn back to it when things get difficult; see it as short-term evidence that you are successfully making a change. Look after yourself, even indulge yourself in other ways, but pick ways that you are confident that you can control, lest you end up doing nothing more than switching addictions. Each time you go through hardship and don't flee into a comforting behaviour is a strengthening of your mental stamina.

Definition: Switching or Addiction Switching
Addiction switching is the act of reducing one addictive behaviour or substance while simultaneously taking up another, effectively 'switching' to the new addiction. Switching is often seen in people who are, by appearances, making substantial headway in ending an addiction and is often used as a more covert form of relapsing. Switching also heavily suggests a deeper misery or discomfort that someone feels they need to soothe in one way or another.

Response: You have had a bad day. However, other days will only get worse if you decide to try and deal with it by misusing gaming. Look for other ways to be kind to yourself.

'I'm nearly at the end of the level/match/dungeon'
Games are typically divided into sections or sessions of some kind. It could be waypoints, dungeons, fights, levels, chapters, save points, energy allocation and so on. The nature of these is that you will typically need to reach the end of that section in order for your efforts to be logged or saved. Hence the conflict occurs when you are an indeterminate number of minutes away from reaching such a waypoint and now have to go to work/go greet your partner/go to bed and so on.

Part of learning to limit your gaming is to think, in advance, about how long any given section of a game will take you. In truth this is not hard to work out, even where some degree of randomness is present. Players need to realise that all boundaries are limits, not targets. If you have to stop playing after two hours, then you absolutely *do not play beyond two hours*, though any amount less is fine. Consequently, you only begin sections of gaming that you know you can finish or that you are prepared to quit before time is up.

Starting sections of play without due planning and then arguing to yourself and others that it is OK to run over is just another way of trying to blur the boundaries. Once they are indistinct, they become malleable, and at that point the excessive habits will quickly take over and bend them further out of shape.

Response: You'll have to re-attempt this section another day, not now. You will need to be more careful what you commit to in games to avoid this happening again.

'I'm playing with someone and can't let them down'
Much as with the former attempt to break the boundaries, this is another set-up to failure. If you play online or over networks with other players, then you need to plan ahead accordingly. If entering into a "World of Warcraft" raid will take between 15 minutes to two hours, then don't start one unless you have agreed, within the boundaries, to play for up to two hours. Doing otherwise is immediately a compromise, even if you finish earlier; eventually the deadline will be overrun, unless you are prepared to abort and potentially leave friends in the lurch.

Response: You are letting someone down, but only by starting what you couldn't finish, not by sticking to your boundaries. Avoid beginning multi-player sessions close to your boundary.

'I've been really good recently'
After a prolonged and successful period of moderating or abstaining, this thought will inevitably begin to creep in. It will tell you that, having not played outside of your boundaries for some weeks/months now, it is unlikely to do any harm to just play a little bit longer than agreed today.

This is an invitation to *relapse* and should be seen as the danger that it is. It is within the first 90 days after the decision to cut back or abstain that a relapse is most likely to occur (Alberta Health Services 2013). Consequently, no amount of good behaviour or control within this timeframe warrants a reward of gaming over the boundaries. Beyond this period, an amendment to the boundaries should be considered, but it should be decided by everyone in the household, and never on an internal whim.

Response: You have been good, and that is why things are going well right now. If you decide to break your boundaries, your gaming, others and your emotions will all suffer.

'Just this once'
Similar to *'I've been really good…'* this thought tries to fool us into thinking that if we act inappropriately now, we will somehow be able to *not* act inappropriately in future. Once again, this stems from treating excessive gaming as a reward, which once again needs to be reframed.

   Each time you overstep the boundaries, you make gaming into something more and more negative and, in the long run, something that you will have to increasingly restrict or stop altogether. You will need to learn to respect your hobby by limiting it and not misuse and pollute it until it becomes hurtful.

Response: If you give yourself permission to break a boundary now, what's to stop you doing it again? Your brief indulgence will take away the structure that's keeping gaming healthy and worthwhile.

'I'm not sure what time it is, so I'll keep playing'
The decision to not keep an eye on the time or to play without a functioning clock visible is a mistake in itself. You are failing even before you run over time if you are

not doing so. Always remain aware of time and if you cannot do so, then don't game until you are able to.

Response: If you're not aware of time whilst gaming then you are not gaming mindfully. Stop gaming now and start again when you are more present.

'I was only half-playing; I was actually doing something else'
This thought is going to become more and more prevalent as we move forward. The degree to which we are able to integrate gaming into other activities is set to increase over the next few years due to the increase in mobile gaming and the trend toward using split/multiple screens.

While this will no doubt be highly enjoyable and efficient for many of us, for addicted gamers this offers an acute risk. If our gameplay is made up of a myriad of quick looks toward a screen or periodic button presses while we get on with work or cooking then how are we to be clear about when we are gaming and when we are not? For an addicted gamer, the mere presence and availability of gameplay will mean that it is almost entirely occupying their thought process. This is, in effect, identical to playing directly and just as harmful and degrading to the experience if it is being carried out too much.

If you have a game running or active during another activity, then treat *all* such time as gaming time; if it is within the boundaries you have agreed to, then fine. If not, then stop playing.

Response: If you want to spend your gaming time partially doing other things, that's fine, but it all counts as gaming as far as your boundaries are concerned.

'Checking-in doesn't count as playing'

Appointment-based games, such as "The Simpsons: Tapped Out", encourage frequent, tiny visits that can be less than a minute long. Such games are usually designed such that failing to not check in incurs a penalty. These games can offer a peculiar issue for someone trying to keep their play within boundaries, in that tracking time spent gaming becomes nearly impossible while playing them 'effectively'. More often than not, addicted players of games that invite checking in will play a host of similar games, cycling through them and nudging forward their progress in each one. The processes of documenting and timekeeping that are key to resolving addiction can end up taking as much time as the games themselves, quickly becoming fiddly. Fiddly boundaries are much like complex boundaries – easily abandoned.

An alternate solution to the one presented earlier is to agree that any gaming session counts as lasting a minimum period of time, say 15 minutes. This would mean that each time you game, even for as little as two or three minutes, it gets marked down as 15 minutes. This allows you to check in with your games, encourages you to attend for a decent length of time and avoids the creep of many small trips overtaking your day.

Response: Checking in needs to be treated as a significant chunk of gaming in order to be controlled. You can check in, but if you do, it counts as an agreed minimum block of your gaming time.

'I'll play less tomorrow to make up for it'

While a system of boundaries may well allow room for manoeuvre, and this is fine, no more exchanges can take place outside of these boundaries. If you have agreed that you can play for four hours on the weekend then it is fine to do two hours on Saturday, followed by two hours on Sunday, it is not fine for you to play five hours this weekend on the grounds that you either played for only three last weekend or will only play for three next weekend.

Bargaining such as this has no limit to it. Once you have made it clear that you can 'borrow' from other allocations, there is nothing to say how much this can be done, how frequently or how far in advance. Consequently, it makes the whole system malleable and therefore easy prey for the unconscious to manipulate into once again allowing for excess. It is a form of undermining and to be avoided if progress is to be made.

Response: You can play less tomorrow but that doesn't change the boundaries today or for any other day. Stopping before the boundary today is important in helping you relearn control.

'The boundary is wrong, I should be able to play for longer'
An important illusion to dispel when setting up boundaries is the notion that the amount of gaming that is prescribed is somehow the 'right' amount to game; this is not the case. Boundaries are not an accurate ruling as to how much someone *should* game. The benefit of boundaries is not that gamers are prevented from gaming at times. The benefit is that they provide a structure around which someone can learn how to regain control.

With all of the above, you need to remember that it is the limitation on gaming that makes it enjoyable in a healthy way. For 90 percent or more of gamers, this limitation is comfortably self-imposed. You are one of the few that has to learn to how to impose a limit. Any attempt to break this limit is going to indirectly reduce how rewarding gaming can be.

Response: The boundary is not trying to be right or wrong. It is there so you can exercise control. It should feel wrong to stop; that's what makes it a victory for your self-control when you do so.

Note: It is, as stated in step five, vital that the gamer is involved and helps establish the boundaries with their household. If they did not get this opportunity to help shape the boundaries, then they do have legitimate grounds to call for them to be reviewed.

7. Seek Professional Help

If you have reached this step then you are most likely dealing with addiction. In this case, it is best to implement the rest of the steps. This stage requires you to start to enlist mental health professionals. As with any other mental illness, the best way to start this dialogue with services is to go to your local doctor for an initial consultation. They may well be able to give clear and useful direction. Taking their suggestion into account, you should then go on to investigate and put in place some form of therapeutic relationship for the gamer.

There are a number of counselling options available that are considered effective in counteracting gaming addiction and its triggering distress (King 2011). It is important to get such a relationship in place as quickly as possible once you know that you are dealing with addiction. As the band-aid of gaming is taken away, a host of emotional sores and wounds will be revealed; having someone who is trained to hear and shoulder these feelings in confidence is vital. As with all counselling relationships, it is equally important to ensure that the gamer feels like he has a good rapport with the professional involved. If they don't – if confiding and trusting are not coming easily – then change to someone else.

Cognitive-behavioural therapy (CBT) is frequently recommended for addiction and can work effectively. The only potential trap with goal-focused therapies such as CBT is that the counsellor can end up focusing solely on stopping the problematic gaming without attending to the disturbances that led to it. If it is accelerating the pace at which the gaming decreases without providing the room to hear the ensuing distress, it is likely to get spat back out by the gamer. Motivational interviewing, also recommended by research, comes with a similar caveat.

Definition: CBT

Cognitive-behavioural therapy, for the few left that don't already know. In the last 10 years this one school of counselling and psychotherapy has become the most dominant model of practice. This is not without good reason, as much of the research implies that it has the highest rate of success, though this is a strongly contended issue. CBT works on the basis that our thinking can be faulty and if we can correct that we can improve our mental wellbeing.

Outside of CBT you have a wide range of other counselling styles. The flipside of the CBT problem can manifest here, in that it is easy to find a counsellor/psychotherapist who creates a powerful sense of trust and emotional caring, but applies little pressure towards the goal of controlling the gaming. This is fine, assuming that there is some other force in the gamer's life, such as family or another treatment programme that is actively working to rein in the level of play. This is not to say that such a relationship won't have its merits, but it is unlikely to have any impact on the gaming any time soon.

Family therapy is well worth considering. This is particularly relevant in households where the gaming addiction appears to be the single major obstacle faced by a family. As mentioned earlier, people should be aware of the possibility of scapegoating. Every case of gaming addiction I have worked with has been set against the backdrop of a troubled domestic life. I would therefore urge people who find themselves in relationship with an addicted gamer to look at themselves as much as the gamer – book yourselves in as a household with a family/couple counsellor, at least for four weeks, to acknowledge everyone's potential part in the situation. This can improve the situation in a number of ways, particularly in helping the gamer to avoid feeling like he's been singled out.

Counselling and psychoeducational groups are a fantastic resource if there is one available, particularly if they are targeted at the issue of gaming. Such groups may focus on either addicted or problematic gaming – I would say that any such group would be worth considering as they would all share the same goal. Not only do they provide the emotional support required, they also offer a sense of community and disband the isolation that people can feel when they are in the depths of addiction. Another quality of groups is that they allow the gamer to begin flexing their social muscles in relative safety, creating opportunities for genuine face-to-face contact under the supervision of professionals.

Groups are often built around the 12-step programme, which, as I outlined earlier, works from a very different premise to the approach I use here, the key differences are as follows:

- The addiction is considered a disease.
- The gamer needs to come to an acknowledgement that they are powerless to change the addiction alone.
- The gamer is asked to draw upon a spiritual or religious resource.
- The goal of the work is to stop gaming altogether.

12-step programmes, like any therapy, work providing they feel right to the gamer themselves. If they attend and feel like they are genuinely benefitting from the approach then by all means stick to it. While the approach presented by this book is a moderation-based approach, it can still run concurrently with such programmes, though I would advise using these resources when it becomes clear that the gamer simply cannot play in a healthy way. If you do look for a group then find one where the gamer feels safe and hopeful – that is a great indicator of its future effectiveness.

Definition: Moderation

Moderation is the process of limiting an addictive behaviour or substance such that it no longer impacts negatively on a person's life. Where video game addiction is concerned this is achieved, typically, through drawing up a set of adhered to boundaries that dictate how frequently and under what conditions the gamers get to game.

8. Go Public

Secrecy is the boiling pot within which the majority of mental illnesses are cooked up; when a problem is covered over, hidden away or not talked about it starts to breed and magnify, worsening the situation far beyond its initial scope. This is a particularly powerful factor in gaming – as we have said before, as an activity it is remarkably safe and also easy to perform in solitude. When a person in distress is left to use gaming in order to manage their difficulties away from others the problem is more than likely to escalate. It is crucial that they begin to make others aware of their gaming, how they are using it and how often. When we acknowledge our behaviour to others, even if those others are not being directly critical, we are forced to acknowledge our behaviour to ourselves.

Start by bringing all gaming into a public space. This will require some creative thinking given the nature of the gaming and the realities of the living arrangements. Some suggestions would be putting games consoles in the lounge, setting up PCs in communal office space or at the back of the main living area. Perhaps make a rule that devices are restricted to communal rooms and not to be taken off to bedrooms – ensure that the whole household adheres to this (and buy alarm clocks for those that rely upon their phones to get up in the morning!).

Clearly this will come with a host of tensions – such as when the gamer is forced to endure the sound of the television when they want to be hearing the audio of their roleplaying game in the same room. Tensions such as these are often the manifestation of pre-existing difficulties in relationships that have been driven underground by the original and more secretive set-up of gaming. Bringing them out in the open can start to reignite the difficult interactions that were being initially avoided, allowing them to potentially process and repair.

Beyond these steps, make sure that the problem is made clear to the household. Once a gamer has admitted that they are struggling they should also approach their online gaming friends and let them know what's going on – they are ironically, though not surprisingly, a powerful source of encouragement and support. Making others aware not only creates a network of help and assistance, but also allows the gamer to gain a sense of how much they are gaming. Gaming alone, it is difficult to keep track of time. Gaming in public, it is difficult to not do so – especially when your little brother's favourite TV show is on in half an hour and they are sat right next to you reminding you that you need to finish soon.

9. Reach out to Others

For those gamers that choose to play in order to avoid the social world, a crucial goal is to develop their confidence in being with others. As with other reasons for excessive gaming, once the gamer has acknowledged that they choose to game rather than face the object of their distress they have already achieved a considerable success; they now understand gaming as a running away rather than a goal. From here they need to come to terms with the vagaries of socializing by practicing being with others face-to-face.

Strengthening confidence in social situations requires immersing ourselves into relationships that we would previously have avoided. This can be done gradually and across a scale of risk. Taking the plunge into situations that are overly exposing is rarely a useful course of action; for example going for a six week holiday with a group of people we don't know or doing a presentation to our classmates. This kind of overcompensation can work, but it can also drive people back in on themselves, underlining the potential beliefs that they are unwanted by others. Ideally steps should be incremental, always providing safety whilst applying a degree of discomfort and pressure.

Therapeutic groups of problematic gamers and similar online communities can again work well here. They are an excellent way to start easing into new groups where people are comparatively open and undefended about their weaknesses. Often these groups will generate a camaraderie that will start to allow the members to reap the benefits of being valued by others. Gaming addiction clinics often assemble groups of gaming addicts for week-long retreats, creating a safe and boundaried environment in which they frequently form powerful connections with the other attendees.

If counselling groups or retreats are not an option, then the gamer should begin to take on situations that are challenging without being overbearing. It is a good idea to focus on activities that involve a focus outside of the socializing itself, such as sporting or team based activities as outlined previously. Other forms of alternative gaming can be used, if they are of interest to the gamer, such as card games, tabletop war gaming or roleplaying, all excellent ways to build confidence with others without having to tackle socialising head on.

Gradually the challenge of situations should be increased as the gamer becomes more comfortable conversing and forming relationships. The goal here is to start to generate a sense of self-belief such that they reinterpret themselves as a worthwhile person that others benefit from being around. By bringing them into more meaningful contact with others they can also start to increase their levels of empathy. This will, in turn, begin to show that the majority of people spend much of their time feeling inadequate and that the rest of the world is not without feelings of self-doubt and inadequacy.

The gamer can begin to learn that it is the nature of being that we can never know what the other is thinking, or how we are coming across in their eyes – becoming accepting, even welcoming of this is critical to gaining confidence in social situations.

10. Review

Relapse is a frequent reality in the recovery process for any kind of addiction. For someone to be addicted they will, by definition, find the process of restraining from their console, device or PC to be incredibly difficult and are likely to have periods of reverting to problematic play. As a result, it is important that after each change is implemented, a point is agreed upon at which the progress will be reviewed. As a rule of thumb, 3 months is a good time frame in which to arrange these reviews. It is in the first 3 months that the likelihood of relapse is highest (Alberta Health Services 2013), after this the chance diminishes over time as the gamer gains a greater sense of being able to control how they spend their time.

Just as when the boundaries are set up, the reviewing process should include the whole household. The goal here is to decide if addiction is still present and should, as before, be carried out by comparing the emotions and behaviours of the gamer against the six signs of video game addiction, as laid out in chapter 2. If all of them are still present, or if a single sign is present to the detriment of the individual or others in their household then the boundary and support system needs to be reviewed. For ease of reference they are shown again here:

The Six Signs of Video Game Addiction

Salience	The gaming has become the most important part of the gamer's life. The majority of their thoughts and desires are now about the game.
Mood Modification	The gamer's emotional state becomes heavily influenced by gaming to the point whereby they appear to need the game in order to feel normal.
Tolerance	The gamer is never satisfied by the games; either perpetually playing the same game or constantly cycling through many different games.
Conflict	The gamer finds themselves frequently arguing with or trying to deceive others when it comes to the subject of their gaming habits.
Withdrawal	When the gamer finds themselves cut off from playing they suffer from negative emotional states such as irritability, sadness or anxiety.
Relapse	The gamer has previously made attempts to control their gaming, either with or without the support of others, but has always reverted back to excessive gaming.

If the review establishes that the signs of addiction are no longer being substantially met, or that they have greatly reduced, then the gamer can be left to manage alone for the next three months. Arrange another review and see how things go until then. This gives the gamer the room to start to act more autonomously and hopefully settle into their own more personal rhythm of gaming. It may well be the case that this then leads to a relapse, in which case it might be agreed that a system of boundaries needs to once again be reintroduced.

If the gamer has repeatedly relapsed, broken boundaries or avoided professional support then a new formula needs to be created – one that involves substantial change. Recalling the recovery message: *'What I've been doing so far to control it has not worked. I need to make a radical change.'* Revisit previous steps, alter the boundary system, review the professional help being used and begin the next three months.

Many gamers will settle into a prolonged form of the 'binge-purge cycle' where they will indulge in excessive gaming for a period of days, weeks or even months, before feelings of game-related self-loathing lead them to stop for a further protracted period. During this time of fasting from video games, they will then start to be drawn back to gaming until they once again begin to play. It is worth noting that this cycle may well work in a relatively healthy way for many gamers – it might become the natural process through which a person manages to strike a balance between their passion for gaming and the acknowledgement that they cannot neglect life away from the screen. We shouldn't forget that gaming is a passionate hobby; for someone to get hugely involved in a game for a period then disengage and do other things is, in itself, not problematic.

However, in order to see if a gamer's cycling between binge playing and then a purge-like quitting is unhealthy, you need to consider whether or not this cycle still contains the other elements of addiction: salience, mood modification, tolerance, withdrawal and conflict. If it does, then it can be viewed as unhealthy. Perhaps it is a step on the way to a more healthy way of living, but if you are in this situation, then you still have further to go. The key here is to distinguish between someone settling into a healthy enough pattern of alternating between gaming and not gaming, as opposed to someone failing to shake off a damaging addiction.

Abstention

Stopping an activity entirely is an admission that you are no longer, as an individual or as a household, able to moderate the behaviour. While abstention should be a last resort, it should also be considered as a continuation of the recovery message. Effectively, you are acknowledging that systems of moderation, no matter how you attempt them, do not work. Once a number of substantial three-month attempts have been made toward moderation it is time for more drastic action.

For some extreme cases, abstention will be the only solution. This is particularly the case for gaming addicts who find themselves, even after prolonged periods of not gaming, unable to simply 'have a game' without immediately becoming addicted again. Much like the worst case scenario of alcoholism, some people will find that upon returning to a game, they cannot but go back to playing to excessive, life-swallowing levels. In these cases it is best to stop gaming altogether, making it and the loss that comes with it a thing of the past.

Quitting gaming for good should follow the same process as before. A system of boundaries is still being used, though its terms are simpler and bolder. Similarly, the thoughts of resistance will need to be carefully monitored for any sign that the old habit has started to try and re-assert itself.

In order to make abstention as easy as possible, remove all trace of gaming and every available chance of a return. By starving the availability you make it far more difficult for addiction to re-establish itself. The ways in which you can and should go about this vary from case-to-case. What follows are some steps that are worth considering. They may also springboard further ideas that might work well in a particular gamer's situation:

- Delete characters from MMOs such as "World of Warcraft" and other role-playing games.
- Uninstall games from all computers and devices.
- Erase accounts with online gaming platforms such as "Steam". You'll need to contact their support team to do so.
- Block access to gaming sites such as "Kongregate". This can usually be done through your operating system (e.g., Windows).
- Get rid of all game-only devices such as consoles and handhelds.
- Get rid of all games and game related paraphernalia, such as magazines, controllers, cases and strategy guides.
- Make sure that everyone else knows that the person is quitting gaming, particularly friends in the gaming worlds themselves as well as any contacts they may have on gaming forums.

- Significant others and close friends that play games as a hobby should refrain from doing so in the company of the abstainer.
- Social events in which games are likely to be played should be avoided.
- Restrict account control on devices so that only a significant other can choose what applications are downloaded. Consult with your device manufacturer for information on how to do this.

Definition: Online Gaming Platform
This is effectively a website through which you can stream and play games that are provided on the site, either freely or for purchase. Many of these sites contain quick and disposable games such as "Armor" and "Kongregate". "Steam" is an increasingly popular platform that provides a wide range of more hardcore games. There are plenty of signs that this will become an increasingly popular way of gaming moving forwards.

Where abstention is the goal, more than ever the presence of professional help is recommended. Institutions such as the Smith & Jones clinic in Amsterdam, or the Centre for Internet Addiction based in Bradford, U.S., are two of a growing number of recovery centres that will contribute in a powerful way to the final and complete abandonment of the need to play video games. Where you cannot access a video game addiction centre or therapist, a non-specialist counsellor or addiction group is still preferable to having no support.

Watch for Addiction Switching
A common tendency for people trying to give up one

addiction is to start another. While the amount of gaming might reduce, there may be an inversely proportionate increase in the use of other habits as a way to fill in the gap that is left behind. The new behaviour can end up taking on the six signs of addiction (albeit in a slightly different guise than those presented here) and become just as problematic as the gaming, possibly even more so.

Switching is an intuitively obvious risk in addiction. When someone who has been addicted finally reduces their harmful behaviour, they find themselves exposed to all the hurts that they have hitherto been anaesthetizing against. Often this will feel like a painful boredom, one that leaves them fidgeting, directionless and unable to commit. They are freshly experiencing the pain of being alive, one that they have been hiding away from. Alternatively, they may be newly exposed to a dangerous or threatening world, one from which they would rather run. Whichever scenario, if the commitment to not game holds, then there is a chance that they will turn to a new form of soothing behaviour, much like their gaming.

The range of new behaviours that could be switched into is huge; addictions take many forms, including both substance and 'behavioural' addictions. The former includes smoking, drinking, caffeine and illegal drug usage. The latter has a broad range that captures exercise, sex, eating, gambling, social networking, work, driving, television, relationship/s, risk taking, criminal behaviour, masturbation, pornography and direct self-harm. While there is an arguably finite list of what can be used as an addiction, it is more worthwhile to look for the six signs repeating themselves and then to find out the associated habit, rather than becoming potentially hyper-vigilant to the myriad of possible addictions.

Often it is not as clear-cut as one in/one out. More commonly someone will, after having left one dominating behaviour, move into a period where they flit across a range of the above behaviours, eager to avoid the pain of simply being. Unless the new behaviour is directly dangerous (such as taking heroin), this is not a bad sign – it shows that something has shifted. The important thing here is to maintain awareness that these are all potentially addictive behaviours. No one substance or behaviour should be allowed to dominate. At reviews, the gamer and their household should bring up any concerns about possible new addictions. If there is any evidence that they are becoming intrusive and harmful, then boundaries and support should be duly arranged.

One of the most obvious 'switches' to look out for involves changing one device for another, thereby never really stopping the addiction to gaming. This is a particular problem with mobile phones and tablets, both of which can serve as a 'second best' gaming platform for addicted gamers when their primary method of playing is unavailable. Nearly every gaming genre you will find on laptops, PCs and consoles has its counterpart on mobile devices. Even genres that are clearly ill-suited to the small screen and limited controls such as first person shooters and role-playing games have numerous incarnations in the various mobile app stores. Much of the reason for this is that gamers who are a fan of a particular play style will tend to use phones as a way to remain attached to their habit even when they are forced to be out and about. In many ways, this is part of the wider appeal of phones; they offer a lifeline to coping strategies that we would otherwise have to cope without.

Additional Suggestions for Loved Ones

If someone you care deeply about has become increasingly lost into the world of gaming, you can find yourself in an unpleasant and lonely place. One of the hardest aspects of this situation is that you will undoubtedly end up having to sacrifice time with your loved one in order to be liked by them. In other words, you'll have to choose between angering and upsetting them by insisting that they come out of their gaming world, or settling for the easy but alienated life of watching the back of their engrossed, gamer head.

While much of your work will be supporting the gamer to implement the steps mentioned above, there are a number of additional actions you can take that will greatly help the gamer:

Give Regular Affirmation and Encouragement

Nearly everyone that ends up addicted to video games is dealing with a poor self-image. As a result, it is vital to regularly do what you can to bolster their perception of themselves. Whenever they stick to their boundaries, or they do something particularly well, tell them so. Should they act unacceptably, focus on the behaviour that you didn't like; avoid making any sweeping statements about them as an individual. Above all make sure you take time to tell them how important they are to you and how much you care about them. The more they feel valued by those close to them the easier it will become for them to value and feel comfortable with themselves.

One of the best ways in which you can give a strong sense of affirmation, particularly with children, is to remain strong for them when they are showing weakness. While it is important that you communicate when you are upset, angry or afraid for them, avoid behaviours that imply that you can't handle these feelings, such as losing your temper, breaking down into uncontrollable tears or simply abandoning/ignoring them. All these types of actions are, amongst other things, immediate and short-term manipulations. They also have the effect of telling the other person that you cannot cope with what they are going through. When you are a parent this is notably perilous; children look to their parents to learn a sense of inner strength in coping with the world. If they do not see it in you they will not develop it internally. Show them that you can handle the feelings that they struggle with and they will grow to follow suit (Bowlby 1988).

All of the above behaviour can be incredibly difficult when your child or loved one is ignoring you routinely, responding aggressively whenever you speak to them and rarely if at all showing that they think highly of or care about you. Living with someone who is acting like this is hard, hard work, particularly if you also struggle with your own self-image. Make sure that you have the right support around you in order to be strong for the other. This might involve your own plan of care for yourself – you may also need to see a mental health professional. The more confidence and self-worth you can muster the more you can provide the affirmation that will help the gamer to break out of their habit.

Model Controlled Behaviour
Review your own lifestyle before you embark on trying to help someone with their addiction to games. Do you have your own poison? Consider all forms of addiction. Do you use another form of excess to hide or indulge in? Unless you are displaying a lifestyle that is free from using

excess as a coping mechanism, you are going to be implicitly endorsing the gamer's addiction.

Make it Clear How the Gaming has Affected You
Tell the gamer exactly what your life is like on account of their gaming habits and how bad things have become for you. This is infinitely more useful than attacking them or predicting how bad their life will be in the future; you are giving them something real. '*You game so much, I no longer feel like I'm married*', '*It's disheartening to see you fail at school because you're too busy gaming*', and '*You've spent over half my earnings this year on games*', are all examples of how the effect of gaming addiction can be made clear to someone. You're not jumping to conclusions or judgements, you're simply telling them what it is like to live alongside their gaming. This kind of realisation is frequently a powerful catalyst for addicts.

Try to communicate your feelings of rejection and concern without letting them overwhelm you into breaking down, becoming angry or walking off. If you succeed, then you are making the effect of the gaming known without scaring or upsetting the gamer back into gaming.

One of the most powerful ways to do this is to write them a letter that simply explains how you've been affected, how it has made you feel and what actions it has driven you to contemplate. Avoid any judgements; keep it about your feelings and the gamer will be unable to merely deny it or write it off as an attack.

Some people are not lucky enough to have a loved one who is bold enough to make us realise just how much they are being hurt. If you don't confront the gamer directly, you will more than likely cook up a crisis in order to get your point across. You might have an affair, lose your temper and strike out or allow bankruptcy to indirectly announce that something has to change. One of the most common ways to make your feelings known is to simply leave the relationship. These are the extremes to which people are unconsciously prepared to go when they don't feel they can get heard. If the gamer can be made to acknowledge the effect that they are having before crisis occurs, that is a good thing.

Care about the Gamer through their Games
If your husband has forfeited spending time with you every night for the past week in favour of playing "GTA V", then there is a huge temptation to treat the game as your enemy; redirecting your sense of hurt and rejection that you feel toward him into the game. Not only does this avoid your real feelings, but it also serves to run down the other person. By attacking their games as stupid, childish, a waste of time, etc., you are, in turn, making a comment about them and thereby further reducing both their self-confidence and your relationship.

If a loved one is engrossed in gaming, then make sure you show an interest in their hobby. Without doing so, you are in a weak position to even begin talking about them – you're relegated to the 'you don't get it' bin. You've also cast a vote against that person: by shutting out someone's interest you are shutting out the person, to some extent. Anything you suggest or venture on the topic is already going to be starting from a discredited position. Conversely, when you express an interest in the games, when you demonstrate a genuine desire to understand what is going on within them, the gamer will feel closer to you and more likely to hear your concerns.

In showing that you have an understanding of the game, you show an understanding of the gamer.

An additional benefit of understanding the other person's games is that you will be in a better position to negotiate with the gamer when it comes to maintaining boundaries. If you know that a raid in "Clash of Clans" takes no more than four minutes, you are not going to be swayed by someone taking fifteen minutes because they are 'just finishing this raid'.

Take the time to find out about the game, what's going on in it and what they are trying to achieve. You might even take part and play the game yourself. All of this serves to take the secrecy and isolation out of the behaviour and shows the depth of the care that you have for the other person.

Don't Be Tyrannised by the Need to Be Liked

Focusing on not upsetting someone or staying on the 'right side' of them is for your benefit, not theirs. One of the six signs is conflict. This is frequently expressed as arguments over how much the gamer is gaming. Certainly with teenagers, much of a parent's role is to show them that you're ok with whatever emotions they throw at you. You might bend, but you won't break, and you certainly won't give up on them. Letting them get their way from time-to-time is important to allowing them to become an adult, but surrendering all your attempted boundaries because you can't handle their sulking or raging is effectively giving up on them.

Sometimes it can feel like a relief to have your angry, upset son divert his attention from attacking you to playing on his PC for days at a time. You might be tricked into thinking that being shut away in his room is what he wants, so it must be what he needs right now. For many young people, the act of hiding away is at the same time both a protest against the hardships of growing up and a plea for someone to come and show that, despite everything, they still love and care for them. Don't be lulled into thinking that just because someone has run away from you, they don't want you to run after them. In the words of Donald Winnicott, '*It is a joy to be hidden but a disaster not to be found*' (Winnicott 1963).

This can equally apply to partners and friends of gamers. When relationships become strained, there can be a sense of relief if they start to spend all their time shut away between headphones and behind doors. The aggravation of the household is hidden away, perhaps for hours. Compared to the hardship of wrestling their attention away from the game this can be bliss, particularly if they need the game to feel OK (mood modification) and react badly to being pulled away from it (withdrawal). The best thing you can do for them (and for yourself if they mean a lot to you) is to be clear to them that you will not settle for this. While you will be made into the bad guy and the peace-breaker here, you will be expressing a genuine care in the relationship. From there they either work with you to effect the steps shown in this book or you both go to couples/family counselling or both.

Parents: Aim to be Good Enough, Not Perfect
Don't get caught up trying to be a perfect parent. Any system of boundaries you create will undoubtedly annoy your child in some way, and if you are to leave them to their own devices (pun intended), they'll most likely still find a way to be upset with you. Concentrate on doing

something instead of nothing, and remember that you are aiming for good enough, not perfect. If your child keeps finding ways to override your boundaries remember that by remaining consistent with your concern you will leave them with a message of care that will stay with them as they grow older.

Parents (again!): Present as a United Front

How much your son/daughter should game is almost certainly going to be a subject upon which you and your partner are going to be divided. Typically one of you will be 'softer' and wanting to go easy on them and the other will be 'harder' wanting to clamp down on the gaming. If you are normal humans, then you will most likely have exaggerated your points of view in order to try and bring about a more acceptable middle ground.

However much you disagree, make sure that when you finally come to talking to your child you are in accordance. Do not hint or suggest that you do not agree with the other parent when in the presence of your child. To do so is to create a division that the addiction will invariably exploit. A child struggling to limit and control themselves needs solid boundaries, if they see one parent laying down the law and another being sceptical they will undoubtedly side with the latter. This makes any system of boundaries malleable, instantly rubbishing it. It also allows the craving child to distract from the gaming by driving a wedge between you and your partner, causing further stress in the household. Take the time to do your arguing and compromising away from your offspring. When you finally present to them, do so clearly and without ambiguity.

Additional Suggestions for Health Professionals

As a counsellor or mental health professional working with gaming addiction there are a number of considerations to bear in mind when working with gaming addiction. While some of the following is from my own experience in counselling, much of it is attributable to a research study by James Driver on recovering gaming addicts, yet to be released at the time of this book's publishing.

Create Safe Conditions for Expression

Many of the young gamers I have worked with had hidden away in a world of gaming partly in order to avoid a relationship in which they felt powerless. Frequently, such clients will find themselves storing up resentment to their parents. Rather than expressing it in a healthy way they subvert the connection to the other by gaming in lieu of spending time with them.

In such instances, it is particularly important to allow the young person the right conditions in which they feel that they can safely show how they feel without fear of repercussions. To do this requires making the boundaries of confidentiality explicit and ensuring that the relationship with the client is clear and as unpolluted by contact with their parents as possible. It is important that this is communicated to the young person, and that they have no sense of communication going on between the parents and the health professionals that does not include them.

Know your Personal Judgements about Gaming

As a therapist or mental health worker, you naturally have to deal with people throwing up issues around which you have negative judgements. Gaming is a frequent candidate for this. There is still a powerful stigma towards gamers and their hobby, particularly from generations that grew up in the absence of video games. Alternatively, you may be positively disposed towards games, so much so that a person in front of you that is crying out to give up gaming keeps being rebuffed by your quest to validate your own pastime and related sense of worth.

James Driver's research showed a number of young people to be resistant to therapy and recovery services due to the stigma that they felt they encountered in therapy. This stigma becomes a barrier to building a relationship. It is the responsibility of the therapist to pay particular attention to their own attitudes around gaming and ensure that they don't have an undue influence over the work. Work them through overtly with a supervisor and not covertly with the client.

Balance the Focus between Gaming and External Pressures
A tension that was thrown up by James Driver's investigations was that some clients became frustrated by their counsellor's focus on arresting time spent gaming at the expense of exploring the difficulties that they faced away from gaming. Equally, many clients encountered the reverse, whereby therapists would spend the whole time exploring external pressures but give little or no help with the practicalities of reducing the gaming.

By making the entire process about limiting or stopping gaming you can miss addressing the problematic issues, be they social, internal or physical, which keep the gamer stuck in their behaviours. If the client's coping strategy of gaming is dismantled or reduced, then either another coping strategy, a change of circumstances or a new skill set needs to be implemented to fill the gap left behind. In addition, you need to respect that for many addicted gamers, the games themselves are still a valuable source of joy and self-expression; overly focusing on their reduction or cessation can alienate passionate gamers.

Conversely, if you are to place too much emphasis on their emotional distress away from gaming, this can be equally frustrating. They might not be aware of it and, given a client's ability to buck any theory we may have, it may not even be there. For many people who game too much, the gaming has become the scapegoat for all the issues in their life. They see that if the problem of gaming was to be removed, then everything else would be manageable. Whether they are right or wrong isn't relevant here, what is important is that if they find themselves with someone who is insisting on focusing on problems that they don't feel they have they will quickly disengage. Stay with the client's position of reducing the gaming, but keep a gently probing attitude alert to the possible emergence of an underlying unease.

Encourage a Mindful Relationship with the Body

With gaming's heavy emphasis on cognition, you will benefit the work and the client by encouraging greater contact with the body. By using body scans, mindfulness and frequent questions about physical movements and sensations you can begin to regenerate a rapport between the gamer's mind and body, enabling them to become more attentive and aware to the needs and pains they may well have been drowning out with games.

Due to the heavily immersive and solvable nature of gaming, players can fidget their way through hours without registering the need to go to the toilet, sleep, eat or rest their aching eyes. For addicted gamers, becoming aware of emotions and bodily sensations will be like an entirely new language for them; I would encourage you to treat it as such. Get them to start knowing how to name and spot their emotions as well as being able to evidence them through reference to the physical sensations they experience throughout their body. Gradually the mind-body relationship will become stronger and the client will begin to better hear and heed their own internal demands.

Understand Games

Lastly, many clients find it difficult to relate to a therapist who doesn't seem to get or understand gaming. This is very similar to the problems faced by many more marginalised groups, such as LGBT clients, refugees or disabled people. The client begins to realise that much of what they are talking about is over the head of the therapist. When they say sentences such as, *'We'd agreed to hit mid and then two of us randomly decided to jungle, leaving me and the other two to get ganked at the second tower'*, you are going to struggle unless you know a little about gaming yourself. In this situation, the therapy sessions can turn into the client having to educate the therapist, leaving them with the sinking feeling that you are never going to 'get it'.

This is not to say that if you are not a gamer you cannot be a therapist on the subject of gaming addiction, just that, firstly, it helps, and secondly, if you are not a gamer, then invest some time into finding out about the games that they are playing. Generally it will be one or two games that really dominate their time so it's a short visit to YouTube and you've learned the basics. Search for 'beginners guide to [name of the game]' and you will quickly learn the nature of the game, the goal of the game and some of its initially baffling jargon.

What Can Video Game Developers Do to Limit Video Game Addiction?

This raises a very difficult question. Is a good game the same as an addictive game? If a studio creates the best game ever are they, by definition, making the most addictive game ever made? Certainly "World of Warcraft" would suggest that this is the case. This has been the dominant game in subscription-based gaming for years and is adored by millions of players. At the same time, it is arguably the game that is linked to video game addiction more frequently than any other. The following section is aimed primarily at people working in the video game industry; I offer an outline for how games can be made that don't unfairly encourage addictive play.

In an article on the responsibility that developers have to their audience, Mark Griffiths cited a number of features of gaming as being correlated with video game addiction. He described these features as character progression, rapid absorption rate and multi-player features (Griffiths 2013). These were the features that showed the clearest correlation to patterns of addicted play in the young people studied.

The difficulty is that these features are integral to certain genres of game. If we were to simply label them as 'bad features' we would be writing off whole swathes of the industry – chiefly all role-playing games and all online games. I would argue that these features, while they might be closely linked to addiction, are more a clue to addictive features, rather than features that are, in themselves, addictive.

Understanding that these suggestions are too broad to take action on, Griffiths goes on to pick out a single, more specific feature that could be altered – reducing the length of quests. Some games' minimum session times, by their very structure, require a time commitment of several hours, instantly forcing the gamer to play to unhealthy levels. In the high-level play of certain MMOs, players often have to commit for several hours or face the recrimination of their team mates. The game is structured in such a way that if you wish to only play for an hour at a time, you will be barred from much of the high-level play. This practice is both detrimental to its users as well as relatively easy to avoid. While some players and groups may choose to overdo their gaming session, it should be the case that were they to only play for an hour a day then all gaming modes and quests would still be worth participating in.

Game designer and blogger Tadhg Kelly takes a more particular issue with the slot machine style of game play, directly relating games' use of the random rewards for empty, skill-less actions as being guilty of creating addiction rather than engagement (the latter being a term he uses for a more healthy compulsion to keep playing). Kelly points the finger at "Mafia Wars" for providing the user with rewards without any actual meaningful play (Kelly 2010).

Jonathon Blow, the creator of the game "Braid", similarly argues against the use of Skinnerian-esque techniques in gaming (Boyer 2007). Specifically, Blow makes the excellent point that it is the scheduling of rewards that is indicative of how unfairly addictive the game is attempting to be.

Nearly every video game involves some kind of reward

system. In "Doom" it involves ammo, new levels and, most importantly, bigger and bigger guns. "Real Racing" gives you money to spend, new races to take part in and, of course, access to newer, faster cars. Importantly, gamers are never given all these rewards all at once, unlike many non-video games, such as chess or football, where everything you will get to use throughout the game is given to you up front; you do not have to score your first goal in a match in order to upgrade your team from 10 to 11 players, for instance. 'Scheduling rewards' is a massive task for design teams that has the following broad aims:

1. To ensure that new players are constantly getting rewarded (creating the rapid absorption rate that Griffiths talked about above).
2. To ensure that long-term players have to wait longer and longer between rewards (effectively guaranteeing that they invest the most amount of time/money for the content they get rewarded with).

As a game designer, I would conduct the reward scheduling by laying out massive timelines. These charts would enable me to see that we were being duly generous to the new user in order to hook them in before relying upon, in retrospect, the 'tolerance' aspect of addiction to allow us to become increasingly mean to players and still retain them as gamers.

Blow's point is simply this: if you strip a game of its reward schedules, is it still fun? If the answer is yes, then you have a game that is fun in a healthy way. If the answer is no, then you are looking at a game that is largely designed to addict players and offers them little else. With this proposal, Blow does an effective job of highlighting how certain games rely upon constantly tantalising the user with the next reward at the exclusion of giving them decent gameplay. Controversially he then goes on to cite "World of Warcraft" as an example of a game that relies upon its reward scheduling over the quality of its gameplay.

Considering Blow and Kelly's thoughts in light of what we know of addiction, it becomes clear that a game that relies more upon providing expectation rather than meaningful, learnable and challenging experience is a game that promotes unhealthy play. Games such as this, particularly where there is no quality mechanic at the heart of the game, are constantly telling players that 'things are about to get good', without ever getting good. Our brief foray into neuroscience would show us that this kind of shallow experience that points to some ever-vanishing nirvana of gameplay is the perfect breeding ground for harmful levels of gameplay.

Games that typify this prioritising of expectation over experience would be the rash of digital collectable card games that began appearing in 2010. These games would literally encourage you to tap the screen in order to get a prize. Games such as these offer a constant treadmill of reward-chasing with next to no depth to the individual quests and battles that largely play themselves. Conversely, "Super Hexagon" is a game that, while having a basic system of rewards, uses its fantastically gripping gameplay as its reason to return.

Finally, it is in the hands of the gaming world to help players be more mindful of the time they are spending gaming. One of the most important steps for addicted gamers is for them to remain aware of the time they are investing. Nintendo already does this as part of its operating systems, but not to any meaningful extent. More notably, "Guild Wars" makes the point of gently flagging up, in game, when you have played for longer than it recommends, highlighting exactly how long your session has been. This kind of care for the gamer should not need to be addressed by individual gaming companies. Instead, I see it as the duty of platforms such as Playstation Network, iOS, Xbox Live and Android to take responsibility for keeping careful track of the time you have spent in front of the screen and notifying you when you are investing concerning levels of time.

The Future of Game Addiction

Gaming will, for the foreseeable future, continue to evolve rapidly to become more accessible, more social, more compelling and more immersive. As virtual reality seems set to make a hopefully more impressive comeback, games will increasingly integrate themselves between our various devices and rumours of a move toward unlimited, atom-based, 3D environments, rather than the constraints of the polygon have been washing about the net for a few years now. All of this points to more accessible and more immersive gaming environments.

Perhaps the most important move will be the improvement in internet connections and subsequent rise of cloud-based gaming, meaning that we will be able to access games as easily and freely as we do music and film with far more capacity to play alongside one another. This will inevitably make games all the more social. As we have already discussed, this will thereby increase the frequency of addictive play. It is interesting to look at the countries in the world that are trailblazing the furthest into this territory, namely South Korea. There, where the internet is widely available at all times across major cities, the issue of video game addiction has led to some severe measures being taken by the government. There is already talk of similar action being taken in the U.K.

We will soon see how things play out in South Korea. I would speculate that it will be similar to other attempts to prohibit potentially addictive habits; people will continue to access them despite having to do so criminally. Still, they are coming up with new and different solutions, and doubtless we will learn something important from it.

While addiction is nothing new, video game addiction is an increasing reality within society. When a soul perceives a threat to its essence, such as lasting pain, the dread of depression or the sense of being useless or unlovable, it will often turn to a pleasurable, affirming or engulfing behaviour in order to feel safe. Once this becomes an entrenched pattern, the fear of a life without the behaviour starts to dwarf the drawbacks of the behaviour itself.

The particular risk of gaming is that the risks are so low. It is only by reference to statistically insignificant extremes that we can point to any real danger at all. As a result, the incentive to put down the tablet/phone/ controller reduces greatly. But this does not mitigate the inevitable loss of confidence, freedom and autonomy that we can suffer in a life spent continually focused on the next opportunity to game. Equally, we cannot ignore the inevitable damage done to relationships when they are sidelined in favour of gaming.

For the parents out there, we find ourselves bringing up children in a digital landscape that is quite unlike the life we grew up amidst. As with all parents before us, our own childhoods are inaccurate templates upon which to navigate our children's path through life. We need to remain vigilant to possible harm being done to the younger generation while having the openness to accept that their ways of interacting with the world will be, by necessity, jarringly different from our own. Let them game, but make sure they game mindfully.

For the spouses and friends of addicted gamers, you have the difficult task of determining what level of gaming you feel is acceptable and what leaves you feeling rejected and unloved. There are no handed down rules of etiquette on the subject. The generation before simply did not have to face the issues in the way you do. Concentrate on your feelings as these are, no matter the issue, unshakably true. Between what is written here and your own honest expression of your emotions you should have what you need to reconnect with someone who has been lost to gaming.

Given time, most addicted gamers will drop the habit on their own. It is the responsibility of game developers, mental health practitioners, loved ones and the gamers themselves to ensure that the damage done before then is kept to a minimum, allowing them to get the most out of life upon their return. For all the fun and wonder that gaming has to offer, it should never be more than a part of our world. A confidence in the body, the intimacy of being next to another and the contentment of a mind at peace with itself form the bedrock of happiness.

BIBLIOGRAPHY

Alberta Health Services, *Relapse Prevention - Planning for Success*,
    10/09/2014 sourced, http://www.albertahealthservices.ca/2485.asp
American Psychiatric Association (2013) *Diagnostic and Statistical
    Manual of Mental Disorders (5th ed.)*, Arlington, VA: American
    Psychiatric Publishing.
Ashliman, D.L. (2003) *Introduction to Aesop's Fables*, New York:
    Barnes & Noble Books
Barnett, J. & Coulson, M. (2010) 'Virtually Real: a Psychological
    Perspective on Massively Multiplayer Online Games', *Review of
    General Psychology 14(2)*
Bartle, R. Players Who Suit MUDs, 10/09/2014 sourced,
    http://mud.co.uk/richard/hcds.htm
Bem, S. & De Jong, H.L. (2006) *Theoretical Issues in Psychology*, Sage
    Publications
Berke J.D. (2000) 'Addiction, Dopamine, and the Molecular
    Mechanisms of Memory', *Neuron (March 2000): Vol. 25, No. 3, pp.
    515–32*
Berridge, K.C., Aldridge, J.W., Smith, K.S., (2011) *Disentangling
    Pleasure from Incentive Salience and Learning in Brain Reward
    Circuitry*, University of Michigan
Reed, B., *Candy Crush Saga Generated an Insane $1.5 Billion in
    Revenue Last Year*, 10/09/2014 sourced,
    http://bgr.com/2014/02/18/how-much-money-does-candy-crush-
    make/
Binswanger, L. (1946) *The Existential Analysis School of Thought, in R.
    May, E. Angel and H. F. Ellenberger (eds) Existence*, New York: Basic
    Books
Bly, R. (1990) *Iron John: A Book About Men*, Rider
Bowlby, J. (1988) *A Secure Base; Parent-child Attachment and Healthy
    Human Development*, New York: Basic Books.
Boyer, B., Leigh, A., *MIGS 2007: Jonathan Blow On The 'WoW
    Drug'*, 10/09/2014 sourced, http://www.gamasutra.com/php-
    bin/news_index.php?story=16392

Csikszentmihalyi, M. (2002) *Flow: The Psychology of Happiness*, Rider

Cuddy, A., *Your Body Language Shapes Who You Are*, 10/09/2014 sourced, http://www.ted.com/talks/amy_cuddy_your_body_language_shapes_who_you_are?language=en

Doan, A.P. (2012) *Hooked on Games, The Lure and Cost of Internet and Video Game Addiction*, FEP International

Ducheneaut, N., Yee, N., Nickell, E. & Moore, R. J. (2007) *'Why Do MMO Players Spend so Much Time Playing Alone?'*, Palo Alto Research Center and Stanford University

Duhig, C. (2012) *Habit: Why We Do What We Do in Life and Business*, Random House

Ferguson, C., *A meta-analysis of pathological gaming prevalence and comorbidity with mental health, academic and social problems*, 10/09/2014 sourced, http://www.ncbi.nlm.nih.gov/pubmed/21925683

Ferster, C.B., & Skinner, B.F. (1957) *Schedules of Reinforcement*, New York: Appleton-Century-Crofts

Fingarette, H. (1988) *Heavy Drinking: The Myth of Alcoholism as a Disease*, University of California Press

Gentile, D., Jones, S. & Ferlazzo, M. (2009) *Pathological Computer and Video Game Use*, Iowa State University

Gladwell, M., (2009) *Outliers: The Story of Success*, Penguin

Griffiths, M. & Hunt, N. (1998) 'Dependence on Computer Games by Adolescents', *Psychology Reports*

Griffiths, M. D. (2008) 'Diagnosis and Management of Video Game Addiction', *Directions in Addiction Treatment and Prevention, Vol 12*

Griffiths, M. D., (2013) 'Social Responsibility in Online Videogaming: What Should the Videogame Industry Do?', *Addiction Research and Theory*

Griffiths, M. D., *Term Warfare: 'Problem Gambling' and 'Gambling Addiction' are not the same*, http://drmarkgriffiths.wordpress.com/2014/07/06/term-warfare-problem-gambling-and-gambling-addiction-are-not-the-same/

Griffiths, M.D., *The Six Components of Addiction*, 10/09/2014 sourced, http://tristanno.wordpress.com/2011/04/22/the-six-components-of-addiction-as-defined-by-mark-griffiths-ph-d/

Griffiths, M. D. *Online Computer Gaming: Advice for Parents*, 10/09/2014 sourced, http://sheu.org.uk/sites/sheu.org.uk/files/imagepicker/1/eh271mg.pdf

Griffiths, M.D., *Video Game Addiction: Further Thoughts and Observations*, 10/09/2014 sourced http://link.springer.com/article/10.1007%2Fs11469-007-9128-y

Humpreys, K. & Klaw, E. (2001) *'Can Targeting Nondependent Problem Drinkers and Providing Internet-Based Services Expand Access to Assistance for Alcohol Problems? A Study of the Moderation Management Self-Help/Mutual Aid Organization'*, Journal of Studies on Alcohol and Drugs

Internet Advertising Bureau, *33 million UK game players*, 10/09/2014 sourced, http://www.iabuk.net/news/33-million-uk-game-players

Internet Advertising Bureau, *UK Digital Adspend Hits Record 6 Month High of £3bn*, 10/09/2014 sourced, http://www.iabuk.net/about/press/archive/uk-digital-adspend-hits-record-6-month-high-of-3bn

Jacobs, M.A. (1971) The Addictive Personality: Prediction of Success in a Smoking Withdrawal Program, American Psychosomatic Society

Jellinek, E. M. (1960) *The Disease Concept of Alcoholism*, Hillhouse

Juul, J. (2013) *The Art of Failure: An Essay on the Pain of Playing Video Games*, The MIT Press

Kelly, T., *Ethical Design: Are Social Games Just Virtual Slot Machines?*, 10/09/2014 sourced, http://www.gamasutra.com/blogs/TadhgKelly/20100126/4239/Ethical_Design_Are_Most_Social_Games_Just_Virtual_Slot_Machines.php

King, D. & Delfabbro, P. (2009) 'Understanding and Assisting Excessive Players of Video Games: A Community Psychology Perspective', *The Australian Community Psychologist*

King, D. L., Delfabbro, P. H. & Griffiths, M.D. (2013a) 'Trajectories of Problem Video Gaming Among Adult Regular Gamers: An 18-Month Longitudinal Study', *Cyberpsychology, Behaviour and Social Networking, Volume 15, Number 1*

King, D. L., Delfabbro, P. H. & Griffiths, M.D. (2013b) 'Video Game Addiction', *Principles of Addiction, Chapter 82*

King, D., Delfabbro, D. H., Griffiths, M. D., Gradisar, M. (2011) 'Assessing Clinical Trials of Internet Addiction Treatment: A Systematic Review and CONSORT Evaluation', *Clinical Psychological Review*

Kranzberg, M. (1986) 'Technology and History: "Kranzberg's Laws" ', *Technology and Culture, Vol. 27, No. 3, pp. 544-560*

Kuchera, B. BBC Article Misses the Point on "Video Game Addiction," Possible Government Legislation of MMOs, 10/03/2014 sourced - subsequently taken down, http://www.penny-arcade.com/

Kuss, D.J. & Griffiths, M.D. (2012) 'Online Gaming Gddiction in

Children and Adolescents: A Review of Empirical Research', *Journal of Behavioral Addictions 1(1)*

Lally, P., Van Jaarsveld, C.H.M., Potts, H.W.W. & Wardle, J. (2009) 'How are Habits Formed: Modelling Habit Formation in the Real World', *European Journal of Social Psychology*

Lemmens S.J., Valkenburg P.M., Peter J. (2009). 'Development and Validation of a Game Addiction Scale for Adolescents', *Media Psychology*

Li, H. & Wang, S. The Role of Cognitive Distortions in Online Game Addiction Among Chinese Adolescents, 10/09/2014 sourced, http://www.sciencedirect.com/science/article/pii/S019074091300 2168

Macguire, P. Compulsive Gamers not Addicts, 10/09/2014 sourced, http://news.bbc.co.uk/1/hi/technology/7746471.stm

MacLean, P.D. (1990) *The Triune Brain in Evolution: Role in Paleocerebral Functions*, New York: Plenum Press

Maltz, M. (1960) *Psycho-cybernetics*, NJ: Prentice-Hall

McGonigal, J. (2011) *Reality is Broken*, Vintage Digital

McLean, L. & Griffiths, M. (2013) 'The Psychological Effects of Video Games on Young People: A Review', *Aloma 31 (1) 119 – 133*

Morris, C. *Free-to-play Set to Take off on Consoles*, 10/09/2014 sourced, http://www.gamesindustry.biz/articles/2013-08-22-free-to-play-set-to-take-off-on-consoles

Nagygyorgy, K., Urban, R., Farkas, J., Griffiths M.D., Zilahy D., Kokonyei, G., Mervo, B., Reindl, A., Agoston, C., Kertesz, A., Harmath, E., Olah, A., & Demetrovics Z. (2013) 'Typology and Sociodemographic Characteristics of Massively Multiplayer Online Game Players', *International Journal of Human-Computer Interaction, 29:3, 192-200*

Nakkan, C. (1996) *The Addictive Personality: Understanding the Addictive Process and Compulsive Behaviour*, Hazelden

Nathan, Peter E. (1988) 'The Addictive Personality is the Behavior of the Addict', *Journal of Consulting and Clinical Psychology, Vol 56(2), Apr 1988, 183-188.*

Office for National Statistics, Alcohol-related Deaths in the United Kingdom, Registered in 2012, 10/09/2014 sourced, http://www.ons.gov.uk/ons/rel/subnational-health4/alcohol-related-deaths-in-the-united-kingdom/2012/stb—-alcohol-related-deaths-in-the-united-kingdom—registered-in-2012.html

Parfitt, B., *UPDATE: The Sun 'Investigation' Claims Gaming is 'As*

Addictive as Heroin', 10/09/2014 sourced,
http://www.mcvuk.com/news/read/the-sun-investigation-claims-gaming-is-as-addictive-as-heroin/0135035

Plato, *Phaedrus*

Poe, E.A. (1848) *Letter to Sarah Whitman*

Ravaj, N. (2006) *How Do Game Events Marking Success vs. Failure Affect a Player's Level of Engagement?*, Helsinki School of Economics, Media Interface & Network Design

Report of the Council on Science and Public Health, 10/09/2014 sourced, http://www.ama-assn.org

Rigney, R., *These Guys' $5K Spending Sprees Keep Your Games Free to Play*, 10/09/2014 sourced, http://www.wired.com/2012/11/meet-the-whales

Robinson, A., *Triple A Consoles Studios 'declined by 80% this gen' says EA exec*, 10/09/2014 sourced, http://www.computerandvideogames.com/417770/triple-aconsole-studios-declined-by-80-this-gen-says-ea-exec/

Robinson, K., *How Schools Kill Creativity*, 10/09/2014 sourced, http://www.ted.com/talks/ken_robinson_says_schools_kill_creativity?language=en

Roger, K., *Candy Crush Addicts Come Clean: 'Life's too Short for Sliding Candies Around'*, 10/09/2014 sourced, http://www.theguardian.com/technology/2014/mar/26/app-addicts-candy-crush-tales

Rosecrance, J. (1985-1986) ' "The Next Best Thing": A Study of Problem Gambling', *International Journal of the Addictions, 20 (11-12), 1727-1739*

Sax, L. (2009) *Boys Adrift: The Five Factors Driving the Growing Epidemic of Unmotivated Boys and Underachieving Young Men*, Basic Books

Schell, J. (2008) *The Art of Game Design: A Book of Lenses*, Morgan Kaufmann

Shaffer, H.J., (2011) *'Overcoming Addiction: Paths Towards Recovery'*, Harvard Health Publications

Siegel, D. (2010) *Mindsight*, Random House

Sky News, *Casual Gaming More Popular Among Women*, 10/09/2014 sourced http://news.sky.com/story/1141502/casual-gaming-mostpopular-among-women

Squire, K. & Intell, J. (2003) 'Video Games in Education', *Games & Simulation*

Thompson, D. (2013) *The Fix*, Collins

Toohey, P. (2012) *Boredom: A Lively History*, Yale University Press

Travis, J. (2003) 'There's no Faking it', *Science News, Vol. 164, Issue 22*

Turkle, S. (2011) *Alone Together: How We Expect More from Technology and Less from Eachother*, Basic Books

Van Cleave, R. D. (2010) *Unplugged: My Journey into the Dark World of Video Game Addiction*, Health Communications

Van Deurzen, E. (2009) *Everyday Mysteries*, Routledge

Wallsten, S. (2013) *What We Are Not Doing When We Are Online*, 10/09/2014 sourced, http://www.nber.org/papers/w19549

Warburton, D.E.R., Bredin, S.S.D., Horita, L.T.L., Zborgar, D., Scott, J.M., Esch, B.T.A. & Rhodes, R.E. (2007) 'The Health Benefits of Interactive Video Game Exercise', *Applied Physiology, Nutrition and Metabolism, August 32 (4)*

Washton A. et al. (1989) *Willpower's Not Enough*, Harper & Row

Watts, A.W., (1951) *The Wisdom of Insecurity*, Pantheon Books

Williams, D., Consalvo, M., Caplan, S., Yee, N., 'Looking for Gender: Gender Roles and Behaviors Among Online Gamers', *Journal of Communication*

Wilson, B. (1939) *Alcoholics Anonymous: The Story of How Many Thousands of Men and Women Have Recovered from Alcoholism*, Alcoholics Anonymous World Services, Inc.

Winnicott, D. (1963) *Communicating and not Communicating*, International Universities Press

Wittgenstein, L. (2009) *Philosophical Investigations*, Wiley-Blackwell

World Health Organisation (1992) *ICD-10 Classifications of Mental and Behavioural Disorder: Clinical Descriptions and Diagnostic Guidelines*, Geneva.World Health Organisation

Yalom, I. (1980) *Existential Psychotherapy*, Basic Books

Young, K. S. (1998) 'Internet Addiction: The Emergence of a New Clinical Disorder', *Cyberpsychology and behaviour 1:237- 244*

Young, K.S. (1998) *Caught in the Net: How to recognize the signs of Internet addiction and a winning strategy for recovery*, New York, NY: JohnWiley & Sons

Zimbardo, G.P. & Duncan, N. (2012) *The Demise of Guys: Why Boys Are Struggling and What We Can Do About It*, Amazon

Zinberg, N. (1986) *Drug, Set and Setting: The Basis for Controlled Intoxicant Use*, Yale University Press

A Gaming Log Sheet

MONDAY

Hours of Gaming	Enjoyment	Comments
		Total Time Gaming